Enhancing Information Use in Decision Making

Peter T. Ewell, *Editor*
National Center for Higher Education
Management Systems

NEW DIRECTIONS FOR INSTITUTIONAL RESEARCH
PATRICK T. TERENZINI, *Editor-in-Chief*
University of Georgia

MARVIN W. PETERSON, *Associate Editor*
University of Michigan

Number 64, Winter 1989

Paperback sourcebooks in
The Jossey-Bass Higher Education Series

Jossey-Bass Inc., Publishers
San Francisco • Oxford

Peter T. Ewell (ed.).
Enhancing Information Use in Decision Making.
New Directions for Institutional Research, no. 64.
Volume XVI, Number 4.
San Francisco: Jossey-Bass, 1989.

New Directions for Institutional Research
Patrick T. Terenzini, *Editor-in-Chief*
Marvin W. Peterson, *Associate Editor*

New Directions for Institutional Research is published quarterly by
Jossey-Bass Inc., Publishers (publication number USPS 098-830), and
is sponsored by the Association for Institutional Research. The volume
and issue numbers above are included for the convenience of libraries.
Second-class postage paid at San Francisco, California, and at
additional mailing offices. POSTMASTER: Send address changes
to Jossey-Bass Inc., Publishers, 350 Sansome Street, San Francisco,
California 94104.

Editorial correspondence should be sent to the Editor-in-Chief,
Patrick T. Terenzini, Institute of Higher Education, University of
Georgia, Athens, Georgia 30602.

Library of Congress Catalog Card Number LC 85-645339

International Standard Serial Number ISSN 0271-0579

International Standard Book Number ISBN 1-55542-849-5

Cover art by WILLI BAUM

Manufactured in the United States of America. Printed on acid-free paper.

Ordering Information

The paperback sourcebooks listed below are published quarterly and can be ordered either by subscription or single copy.

Subscriptions cost $56.00 per year for institutions, agencies, and libraries. Individuals can subscribe at the special rate of $42.00 per year *if payment is by personal check.* (Note that the full rate of $56.00 applies if payment is by institutional check, even if the subscription is designated for an individual.) Standing orders are accepted.

Single copies are available at $12.95 when payment accompanies order. (California, New Jersey, New York, and Washington, D.C., residents please include appropriate sales tax.) For billed orders, cost per copy is $12.95 plus postage and handling.

Substantial discounts are offered to organizations and individuals wishing to purchase bulk quantities of Jossey-Bass sourcebooks. Please inquire.

Please note that these prices are for the calendar year 1989 and are subject to change without notice. Also, some titles may be out of print and therefore not available for sale.

To ensure correct and prompt delivery, all orders must give either the *name of an individual* or an *official purchase order number.* Please submit your order as follows:

Subscriptions: specify series and year subscription is to begin.
Single Copies: specify sourcebook code (such as, IR1) and first two words of title.

Mail all orders to:
Jossey-Bass Inc., Publishers
350 Sansome Street
San Francisco, California 94104

New Directions for Institutional Research Series
Patrick T. Terenzini *Editor-in-Chief*
Marvin W. Peterson, *Associate Editor*

The Association for Institutional Research was created in 1966 to benefit, assist, and advance research leading to improved understanding, planning, and operation of institutions of higher education. Publication policy is set by its Publications Board.

For information about the Association for Institutional Research, write to:

AIR Executive Office
314 Stone Building
Florida State University
Tallahassee, FL 32306-3038

(904) 644-4470

Contents

Editor's Notes

The idea that information is valuable for decision making constitutes a core value of institutional research. It is at the heart of most current training in the profession, and it is embodied in most of the field's rhetoric and professional standards. But research on information utilization as well as accumulated practitioner wisdom continually raise questions about its validity. What preconditions the use of information in decision making in higher education, and how might its utilization be improved? The authors of this volume revisit an old topic in some new ways, reviewing what is known about information utilization on conceptual grounds, then critically valuating some common mechanisms for communicating information to decision makers.

In reviewing what is known about information use, we may find it helpful to distinguish among three distinct topics: organizational contexts, types of utilization, and properties of information itself. Regarding the first, considerable research points out that the utilization of information of all kinds can vary considerably across organizational settings and types of decision makers. In higher education, research has demonstrated that the role played by information in influencing a particular decision may depend on factors as diverse as the formal organization of decision making (Coleman, 1972), the political positions of those generating and using the information (Baldridge, 1971), or the general culture of decision making (Chaffee, 1983). In addition, the disciplinary backgrounds and individual cognitive styles of academic decision makers may profoundly condition their approach to information (Mitroff, 1982; McKenney and Keen, 1974).

The second set of issues concerns the manner in which concrete information enters the decision process. Most formal treatments of the role of information in decision making are based on a rational model of organizational process. But, there is considerable evidence that information utilization is not that simple. Information may serve as a signal to outside constituents that an organization is rationally (and therefore responsibly) administered (Feldman and March, 1981). Negative information in particular can serve to focus scarce administrative attention (March, 1982; Braskamp and Brown, 1980). Finally, information can be used effectively to promote consensus after a decision is made so that coherent organizational action is possible (Brunsson, 1982).

The last set of issues concerns properties of the information itself, particularly the manner in which it is collected and communicated to decision makers. Here, past research on knowledge utilization suggests

1

that the successful application of knowledge requires the simultaneous presence of two conditions. First, the information must have a visible bearing on a perceived problem. Second, there must be a constant and consistent dialogue between those who gather and provide information and those who must use it. Evaluation practitioners, such as Patton (1978) and Coleman (1972), stress the fact that decision makers are often willing to make considerable use of evaluation data that are seen as problem related, even if they are aware that the data are of questionable accuracy. Moreover, it is well known that the ways in which information is actually presented to decision makers can deeply influence whether it is used. Evidence from the evaluation literature suggests that the language in which a particular problem is expressed and the visual formats in which data are presented can have considerable impact on its credibility (Stufflebeam, 1971; Newman, Brown, and Braskamp, 1980).

The first three chapters of this volume set an important context in applying these wider issues to the world of the institutional researcher. All three chapters aim to summarize major findings of past research in other fields with which institutional researchers may be unfamiliar. Thus, in Chapter One I review some major findings on information utilization drawn from the field of evaluation research. In general, these findings can be structured around two key questions for institutional researchers: What does using information really mean? and What affects what actually happens to the information provided? The next two chapters address the second of these questions more systematically by considering two primary contextual factors that strongly condition how information is communicated and used. In Chapter Two, Gerald and Josetta McLaughlin examine the organizational context for information use in terms of the intersections among three levels of managerial activity (strategic, managerial, and operational) on the one hand and five types of informational support activities (selection, capture, manipulation, delivery, and influence) on the other. Then, in Chapter Three, Judith Dozier Hackman reviews the psychological context for information use by applying some lessons drawn from the psychology of individual perception.

The next group of chapters uses these findings to draw some succinct, though generally broad, lessons for practice. One overriding lesson of past research on information utilization can be concisely summarized: context is everything. And, for institutional research in the last decade, contexts have been particularly fluid. College and university missions, clienteles, and administrative arrangements have evolved considerably. While the basic function of institutional research remains one of "provid[ing] information which supports institutional planning, policy formulation, and decision making" (Saupe, 1981, p. 1), the environment in which this function occurs now emphasizes much quicker turnaround in requests for information, and there is consequently less emphasis placed on maintaining a sustained program of research. At the same time, institutional research has been asked to supply an escalating volume of compliance reports for state, federal, and accreditation purposes, and this has somewhat diluted the profession's initial mission of supplying interpreted information for decision support.

Similar fluidity now characterizes the manner in which supplied information enters the realm of policy and decision making. Consistent with the times, discussions of the relationship between institutional research and decision making published in early numbers of this *New Directions* series (for example, Adams, 1977) generally invoked a model of scientific management that emphasized rational policy formulation and formal decision processes. Later volumes (for example, Lindquist, 1981) more often emphasized the quick and dirty, picturing institutional research as a flexible and deployable resource that served a variety of institutional clients and adapted to a rapidly changing environment. More recently still, the analytical/recommendation function of institutional research in decision support has been partially displaced by the function of supplying data directly to decision makers in a form that facilitates their own independent analyses (for example, Stevenson and Walleri, 1984).

Most dramatic of all have been changes in the technology of information itself that directly affect its acquisition, maintenance, and distribution. Improved (but at the same time complex) institutional data bases contain more information about more aspects of institutional operations than ever before, and these are increasingly organized as relational data bases. Commercial statistical software packages, such as SAS and SPSS-X, currently allow analyses and file manipulations that previously required scores of programming hours using third-generation computer languages; these tools render such techniques as transcript analyses and longitudinal student tracking routinely feasible. Most important, advances in microcomputers and in electronic communication promise to alter the traditional institutional balance of power with respect to information in fundamental ways. No longer the sole supplier of decision information, institutional research is increasingly becoming only one of a number of independent players.

The last three chapters of this volume treat these evolving roles from a variety of perspectives. In Chapter Four, Victor Borden and Edward Delaney consider the fact that, for better or for worse, most institutional decision making in higher education is group decision making involving teams, committees, and local units. As a result, lessons from group process and dynamics are particularly applicable if information suppliers are to be heard effectively. In Chapter Five, Larry Jones treats the deceptively familiar topic of institutional research reporting by documenting many changes in the structural and informational environment within

4

which institutional research must operate. He offers some enduring lessons about information presentation drawn from practitioner experience. Finally, in Chapter Six, John Dunn, Jr., examines the impact of new and rapidly changing information technologies, such as distributed data processing and electronic data sharing, on the information function. Together, these chapters provide a foundation for the application of broad lessons about information utilization to some actual predicaments that practicing institutional researchers face. As a conclusion, in Chapter Seven I summarize these lessons in the form of four diagnostic questions that institutional researchers should pose regarding any situation in which information for decision making is requested.

We neither hope nor expect that our treatment of these issues will be definitive. Indeed, one major finding of the research on information utilization is that thinking about the issue is the most important ingredient in addressing it. We hope that this volume will once again provoke practitioners to do so.

Peter T. Ewell
Editor

References

Adams, C. R. (ed.). *Appraising Information Needs of Decision Makers.* New Directions for Institutional Research, no. 15. San Francisco: Jossey-Bass, 1977.

Baldridge, J. V. *Power and Conflict in the University.* New York: Wiley, 1971.

Braskamp, L. A., and Brown, R. E. *Utilization of Evaluation Information.* New Directions for Program Evaluation, no. 5. San Francisco: Jossey-Bass, 1980.

Brunsson, N. "The Irrationality of Action and Action Rationality: Decisions, Ideologies, and Organizational Actions." *Journal of Management Studies,* 1982, *19* (1), 29-44.

Chaffee, E. E. *Rational Decision Making in Higher Education.* Boulder, Colo.: National Center for Higher Education Management Systems, 1983.

Coleman, J. S. *Policy Research in the Social Sciences.* Morristown, N.J.: General Learning Press, 1972.

Feldman, M. S., and March, J. G. "Information in Organizations as Signal and Symbol." *Administrative Science Quarterly,* 1981, *26,* 171-186.

Lindquist, J. (ed.). *Increasing the Use of Institutional Research.* New Directions for Institutional Research, no. 32. San Francisco: Jossey-Bass, 1981.

McKenney, J. L., and Keen, P.G.W. "How Managers' Minds Work." *Harvard Business Review,* May-June 1974, pp. 79-90.

March, J. G. "Emerging Developments in the Study of Organizations." *Review of Higher Education,* 1982, *6,* 1-18.

Mitroff, I. I. "Secure Versus Insecure Forms of Knowing in University Settings: Two Archetypes of Inquiry." *Journal of Higher Education,* 1982, *53* (6), 640-655.

Newman, D. L., Brown, R. D., and Braskamp, L. A. "Communication Theory and Utilization of Evaluation." In L. A. Braskamp and R. Brown (eds.), *Utilization of Evaluation Information.* New Directions for Program Evaluation, no. 5. San Francisco: Jossey-Bass, 1980.

Patton, M. Q. *Utilization-Focused Evaluation.* Beverly Hills, Calif.: Sage, 1978.

Saupe, J. L. *The Functions of Institutional Research.* Tallahassee, Fla.: Association for Institutional Research, 1981.

Stevenson, M. R., and Walleri, R. D. "The Transformation of Institutional Research as a Result of Improving Information Technology." Paper presented at the 24th annual forum of the Association for Institutional Research, Fort Worth, May 1984.

Stufflebeam, D. L. "The Relevance of the CIPP Evaluation Model for Educational Accountability." *Journal of Research and Development in Education,* 1971, 5, 19–25.

Peter T. Ewell is a senior associate at the National Center for
Higher Education Management Systems (NCHEMS).

Information use depends on how use *is defined and on a*
variety of organizational, personal, and presentational factors.
Evaluation researchers have faced and addressed these issues
before.

Information for Decision: What's the Use?

Peter T. Ewell

Institutional researchers are not alone in lamenting the indifference with which decision makers commonly receive the fruits of their labors. As action researchers they share these concerns with a much wider community, many members of which have paid considerable attention to seeking out the reasons for this phenomenon. The most important investigations have probably been those in the field of social program evaluation and in particular in the literature on the utilization of evaluation results. What can we learn from these investigations that we can use to inform the practice of institutional research? With a few caveats, the answer is a great deal, first in broadening our conceptions of the ways in which information is actually used by administrators, then in directing our attention to key factors that affect how and whether information is used. This chapter reviews these two topics, noting some prior treatments of the utilization of institutional research and grounding these discussion in the experience of the wider evaluation tradition.

Institutional Research as Program Evaluation: Parallels and Differences

Like institutional research, program evaluation as a profession can be traced to the early sixties. Large-scale federal programming and the

P. T. Ewell (ed.). *Enhancing Information Use in Decision Making.*
New Directions for Institutional Research, no. 64. San Francisco: Jossey-Bass, Winter 1989.

rise of so-called scientific management techniques, such as **PPBS** and **MBO** (first in the Defense Department, later in various social service agencies), created both a need to determine what was working and a new set of tools that could be used to find out. Based largely on classic quasi-experimental techniques drawn from social psychology (Campbell and Stanley, 1966), the result was a profusion of program impact studies in fields as diverse as primary education, social welfare, distributed health care, and prison reform. However, by the early 1970s, program evaluators were becoming concerned. Too often, "bad" programs seemed to expand, while "good" ones were ignored. In short, nobody seemed to be listening. The result was what Shapiro (1986) has aptly termed "the deconstruction of program evaluation" (p. 166). Practicing evaluators, such as Stuffle-beam (1971) and Stake (1978), began advocating the rejection of study designs that stressed outcomes measurement and experimental controls and promoting more flexible—often "naturalistic"—assessments of process (Guba and Lincoln, 1981). At the same time, evaluators began explicitly and critically examining what was meant by the expression *using results* and discussing proactive strategies designed to promote greater utilization (Patton, 1978).

In drawing lessons from these discussions, institutional researchers must be aware of both identities and differences between the evaluator's profession and their own. Certainly, the two have common roots in their use of empirical, often quantitative, techniques and in their conviction that the results obtained should directly guide managerial action. Moreover, they share a strong conviction about the special role of the action researcher in the decision process, a role that must be accountable both to the decisional needs of the organization served and to the professional standards of research. In their traditional assignments, both evaluation researchers and institutional researchers must maintain independence; they must recognize and subscribe to Saupe's (1981, p. 8) maxim that, "just as the results of the research will seldom be the sole determinant of the decision, so the desired decision cannot be allowed to bias the nature of the research."

The organizational context of the institutional researcher is considerably more organic and flexible than that of the program evaluator. First, the primary unit of analysis for an institutional researcher is only rarely an identifiable program and its intended effects. As a result, such goal-based methods as explicit hypothesis testing or quasi-experiment, which constitute the core of traditional evaluation practice, are rarely applicable in higher education. Even in such areas as academic program review, where in principle goal-based techniques are appropriate, formal studies of program effectiveness remain rare. Most review processes instead employ an alternative evaluation paradigm stressing descriptive data and peer judgment over explicit outcomes measurement (Wilson, 1987).

Moreover, in contrast to the program evaluator, the institutional researcher is an insider. With respect to information use, this means that at the very least, there are considerably more opportunities. Information-laden communication with decision makers is more likely to be continuous and informal and, in the evaluator's language, more formative than summative. Moreover, much of the substance of this communication is likely to be about operations and not outcomes—the real world of decision makers. Supplying needed operating data reliably on a day-to-day basis thus puts the institutional researcher in a much better position than the program evaluator to communicate data-based decisional recommendations when the occasion arises. Most important, routine contact gives the institutional researcher an invaluable opportunity to become familiar with the tastes and traits of particular decision makers and the organization culture within which they operate. While data gathering of this kind is typically informal, it is often formalized in institutional research discussions as "appraising the needs of decision makers" (Adams, 1977) or "assessing the climate for change" (Buhl and Lindquist, 1981), and it can become as important as primary data gathering in an overall action research strategy. At the extreme, this perspective suggests a proactive change agent role for institutional research reflecting sensitivity to organizational dynamics and emphasizing strategies for promoting information-based action recommendations internally (Terrass and Pomrenke, 1981).

A review of the major findings from the literature on evaluation utilization suggests that the implications of these role differences for institutional research are two. First, for the institutional researcher, organizational and perceptual barriers to information use are fewer and less explicit. Lessons on how to promote communication by increasing issue relevance and the attention paid to data presentation will consequently have enhanced probabilities of success. Second, because the information exchange between institutional researchers and decision makers is more continuous, information use can take many different forms. The forms documented in the evaluation literature may consequently help institutional research practitioners to recognize and promote alternative uses when they do occur and to provide decision makers with the kinds of information most suited to such uses.

Concepts of Information Use

For better or for worse, most formal treatments of the role of information in decision making are based upon a rational model of organizational process. According to this model, those who make decisions seek information in order to clarify the probable consequences of the available courses of action. While information cannot make the decision, it can reduce uncertainty about the alternatives that show the greatest possibility of benefit while incurring the least cost (Raiffa, 1968).

The rational model remains compelling, and, as in other information-based professions, it tends to dominate formal constructions of both program evaluation (Weiss, 1972) and institutional research (Saupe, 1981). In essence, it has three implications. First, information professionals supply decision-relevant information but do not themselves participate in decisions. Second, information professionals are expected to try to supply complete and accurate information about the problem at hand. Third, information professionals are expected to be value-neutral in their approach both to gathering information and to presenting it. In combination, the effect of these three attributes is to render the role of the information professional transparent in any given decision. If decision-makers are rational, the information itself may have considerable impact on the outcome of a particular decision. The manner of form in which it is supplied is not a factor.

Nevertheless, it is well known that decision making in higher education, as in other complex organizational settings, does not really work this way. First, different kinds of institutional cultures can encompass quite different conceptions of what constitutes useful information. For example, Chaffee (1983) describes four alternative decision-making models—formal/rational, collegial, bureaucratic, and political—and outlines their distinct information requirements. Second, regardless of the institutional setting, the rational use of information is constrained in multiple ways. Ewell and Chaffee (1984) identify four such constraints in college and university settings: constraints imposed by incomplete information, constraints imposed by politics, constraints imposed by organizational culture, and constraints imposed by the symbolic need for the institution to take unambiguous action. Such dynamics are particularly observable in the histories of explicit information utilization projects in higher education. In one such multi-institutional project intended to test the applicability of detailed resource allocation and management information, utilization depended largely upon establishing perceived linkages between such information and visible unit-level problems (Baldridge and Tierney, 1979). In another project that attempted to apply information on student learning and development to curricular decisions, utilization was often blocked by differences among disciplinary cultures and by resulting symbolic properties of the information provided (Astin, 1976).

Multiple definitions of utilization began to arise in the evaluation literature when it was realized that policymakers were ignoring the majority of large-scale quasi-experimental studies conducted in the mid seventies—a condition described by Guba and Lincoln (1981) as "the tragedy of nonuse" (p. 3). One response was to sharpen conceptions of how evaluation results actually entered the decision process. For example,

Leviton and Boruch (1983) proposed to distinguish between *impact*—utilization that actually affected the outcome of a decision—and *use*—activities that did not necessarily affect the outcome of a decision. Distinctions of this kind reflected emerging evidence about how decision makers actually reacted to the findings of large-scale evaluations. For example, one empirical study of the ways in which evaluation results were used in federal health policy found that a major theme was the reduction of uncertainty among decision makers faced by complexity (Patton and Associates, 1977). But, beyond noting that the rational paradigm of utilization rarely applies, evaluators have not achieved consensus on what alternative notions of use might look like (Shapiro, 1986). As the current debate between Weiss and Patton on utilization illustrates, they have also not agreed on the degree to which conceptions of use can vary across kinds of decision makers and decision-making communities (Smith and Chircop, 1989).

On what alternative conceptions of the way decision makers use the information that they are given can we base these discussions? Four are worth noting. Each implies a somewhat different approach to data collection and transmission.

Use of Information to Identify Problems. Rather than assessing the particular decisional consequences of a set of known alternatives, information may simply be used to signal the fact that a problem exists. In goal-based evaluation, some approaches stressing this kind of utilization are termed *discrepancy evaluation* (Yavarsky, 1976). These approaches generally involve the formal comparison of the performance targets that were hoped for and the results that were obtained. In institutional research, as Saupe (1981) points out, this effect may often result from the routine provision of descriptive information. In essence, problem identification has to do with the detection of anomalies. Consequently, it requires information that quite clearly signals the differences between what was expected and what was found. This first implies a need for comparative presentation, with a standard supplied by past history (trends over time), by the performance of other similar units or entities (peer comparisons), or by expressed expectations. In the last case, formal "expectations exercises," in which decision makers are asked to supply a profile of the numbers that they expect a given data collection instrument to obtain before it is administered, can be particularly useful. Problem identification also implies a need for simplicity in presentation. Only a few key indicators can be used to highlight discrepancy, and these must be presented in such a way that major differences are readily apparent. Graphic presentation may be particularly effective here.

Use of Information to Set a Context for Decision. Considerable research on business decision making indicates that decision makers place more reliance on suggestive than on decisive information systems

(Churchman, 1975). The objective of a suggestive system is to place a given decision in its proper context, to outline its basic parameters, and, most important, to define the ways in which it affects and depends on other parts of the organization. Information of this kind is rarely sufficient for making a particular decision, but it can provide a basic contextual foundation that informs a range of related decisions and the links among them. In the research on evaluation utilization, such use is often termed *conceptual use* (Rich, 1977). It influences the way in which decision makers think about a problem or issue, but it is not identifiably used to inform particular decisions. Its manifestations are most often found in naturalistic evaluations, which attempt to document holistic processes and activities as fully as possible as they occur. In higher education, information for context setting is most often encountered in discussions of strategic planning or program review. Supplying it effectively will generally imply considerable integration and interpretation—often requiring the grouping of quite disparate kinds of information drawn from many sources around a common issue or problem (Kinnick, 1985). Because it attempts to capture holistic processes or experiences, information strategies best suited to context setting often involve substantial discussion of implications from multiple perspectives and considerable use of verbatim testimony from those experiencing the institution in different ways.

Use of Information to Induce Action. Beyond its use in clarifying the consequences of particular decisions, concrete information can help in the process of coming to a decision. Organizational theorists, such as Simon (1957), have highlighted this effect by observing that confusion between empirical and value questions is a particular obstacle to closure in decision processes in which many parties are involved. In such situations, the addition of concrete data about the problem under discussion may provide a degree of closure that goes far beyond the informational value of the data. In program evaluation, Patton (1978) has noted that decisional outcomes may already be largely decided by the time concrete evaluative information becomes available. Its prime effect is therefore to increase the confidence of the decision makers and consequently their willingness to act. Under such conditions, sensitivity analysis may be particularly helpful as an informational strategy. By supplying the probable range of variation in an available result and by indicating that it lies far from the point that would lead to a different decision, information professionals can often help policymakers come to closure. Approaches stressing multiple advocacy (Ewell and Chaffee, 1984), in which differing contenders use available information to build complete alternative cases, may also increase the confidence of decision makers by ensuring that all points of view have been covered adequately.

Use of Information to Promote or Legitimize a Decision. Once a particular decision has been taken, concrete information can become a powerful mechanism for selling the decision to those whose cooperation is needed in order to carry it out. This use reflects the contention that mobilizing support, not decision making itself, is the premier managerial activity and that information designed to promote the rationality of action rather than the rationality of decisions may therefore be most useful to practicing managers (Brunsson, 1982). The effectiveness of information supplied in this role may have nothing immediate to do with either its accuracy or its bearing on the problem at hand. Rather, the information serves as a symbol that the decision was well taken and makes it possible for opposing parties to cooperate by removing the need for one side to back down. Some of the power of explicit information to accomplish this feat undoubtedly has to do with our distinctive cultural reverence for numbers. Part of it has to do with a collective organizational ethic, which is particularly prevalent in higher education, that basing action on systematically collected information signals a serious, rational approach to decision (Feldman and March, 1981). In the evaluation literature, such usage, which has been termed *symbolic* (King and Thompson, 1981), is deemed an inevitable by-product of operating in a political environment. In higher education, it is particularly apparent in external accountability reporting, a form of activity increasingly characteristic of institutional research. The essence of this category of information use is to maintain organizational and leader credibility. As a result, its prime implication for informational strategy is to ensure face validity in the methods used and in forms of presentation. Particular problems here may be caused by the use of survey sampling or of complex statistical techniques, as decision makers, based on their own experiences, often do not believe the results produced by these methods (Ewell, 1988; Schmidtlein, 1977).

Table 1 summarizes these four conceptions of information use and highlights their broad implications for information strategy. By tailoring the content and format of the information supplied to its anticipated use, institutional researchers can anticipate greater policy benefit.

Factors Affecting Information Use

In the evaluation tradition, information use is generally modeled as a communications process between a professional evaluator who supplies information and a program manager who receive it. Factors promoting effective information use are therefore most often those associated with any communications process: attributes of sender and receiver, the channels used, and the organizational or cultural context within which the communication takes place. Thus, Rich (1981) proposes a two-community paradigm in accounting for the nonuse of evaluation results. Evaluators come from a rational social scientific perspective, while decision

Table 1. Conceptions of Information Use

Information Use	Essential Processes for Decision	Appropriate Informational Strategies
Rational decision making	Assessing consequences of alternative courses of action	Cost-benefit Explicit recommendations with reasons for each
Problem identification	Detecting anomalies	Comparative trend reporting Key indicators Graphic presentation Expectations exercises
Context setting	Making holistic connections Systematizing experience	Face-to-face communication Verbatim records Scenario building
Inducing action	Closing further discussion Enhancing decision makers' confidence	Multiple advocacy Sensitivity analysis
Selling decisions	Establishing wide credibility	Face validity

makers come from a pragmatic, political perspective. Most instances of nonuse therefore can be traced to a communications breakdown between these two quite different perceptual worlds. Shapiro (1986) carries this logic a step further by reviewing the contending metaphors of evaluation, which range from the familiar conceptions of evaluation as information production and organizational strategy—both of which focus on rationality and purposive utilization of information—to less familiar conceptions, such as evaluation as political philosophy (emphasizing the political values of those undertaking evaluation) and evaluation as research paradigm (emphasizing their disciplinary backgrounds in the various social sciences). Both arguments emphasize that utilization is largely a process of cross-cultural communication.

Shapiro (1986) outlines the history of empirical attempts to determine the factors responsible for evaluation utilization by presenting case histories of particular evaluations that attempt to follow the impact of results on subsequent decisions. Other approaches focus on decision makers, organizations, and issues: in the first instance attempting through interviews to determine the ways in which different kinds of decision makers think about information, in the second attempting a parallel analysis of the role of information in the life cycle of a particular organization, and in the third following the development of a particular issue and noting the points at which information enters the discussion. Finally, an intriguing handful of studies has been simulation based—artificially varying such attributes as visible evaluator qualifications, information formats (for example, the use of technical jargon), and other variables explicitly drawn from communications theory (Braskamp and Brown, 1980).

The modeling of information utilization as a communications process is also a strong attribute of discussions directed toward improvement of the utilization of institutional research. For example, Schmidtlein (1977) strongly echoes the two cultures perspective of evaluators in his contention that higher education policymakers and information suppliers live in different conceptual worlds and that the former are therefore inclined to be suspicious of the latter. Sheehan's "three hats" theory (1977) is similar in that it explicitly considers the differing roles and resulting communications problems among decision makers, analysts, and information technicians. Although empirical attempts to understand information use in higher education are more circumscribed, they also are largely organized around such factors. For example, in examining the process of using information on student outcomes in a multi-institutional demonstration project, Kinnick (1985) distinguishes between technical and organizational obstacles to utilization and treats both as modifiers to an otherwise unimpeded flow of information between researchers and decision makers.

Figure 1, which models utilization as a communications process, summarizes four key factors related to information use that can be drawn from these discussions.

Organizational Characteristics. One difficulty with the two-community theory, Shapiro (1986) argues, is its assumption that perfect communication leads automatically to effective information use. This assumption ignores the fact that bureaucracies routinely process and interpret information before it is used and that this processing may decisively shape its implications (Rich, 1981). Here, the realization that information is only one ingredient in the decision process and that constituency satisfaction and a smooth flow of operations are paramount managerial concerns is critically important. The dominance of such concerns can decisively influence the impact of evaluation information. For example, one major finding of simulation studies on evaluation utilization is that results are rarely used (or even recognized) at organizational levels higher than the levels at which they were generated (Lazarsfeld and Reitz, 1975) and that they typically do not cross vertical reporting lines within an organization. In higher education, this finding may have particular bearing on the location of institutional research in the reporting structure. Moreover, as Schmidtlein (1977) points out, governance structures in higher education typically mean that decision making is more diffuse and likely to be based on collegial processes. As a result,

Figure 1. Key Factors in Information Use

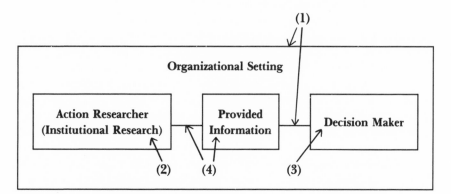

Key Factors:
(1) Organizational characteristics
    Structure of power
    Organizational culture
    Structure of communication
(2) Researcher characteristics
(3) Decision maker characteristics
(4) Informational characteristics
    Information content
    Medium/format

institutional researchers may need to pay particular attention to group dynamics and the use of information in group settings.

Researcher Characteristics. Patton's work on utilization-focused evaluation (1978) pays considerable attention to positive personal characteristics of the evaluator, which include an open, approachable interpersonal style and a maximum of informal communication. Others stress that the evaluator needs to assess the interests, preferences, and styles of decision makers carefully from the outset of the evaluation process. When the information professional is in a permanent staff role, as he or she is in institutional research, the importance of personal characteristics is amplified (Hogan, 1981). Moreover, in group decision-making situations, the need for strong verbal and interpersonal skills becomes paramount.

Decision Maker Characteristics. While the two-community theory emphasizes differences between the cultures and values of decision makers and information professionals, studies of information utilization also reveal considerable differences in the way in which individual decision makers perceive and interpret the same information. Some differences can be traced to the differing cognitive styles of individual decision makers, while others may be the result of differing backgrounds and training (McKenney and Keen, 1974). Because most administrators in higher education were once academics, major differences of this kind may be due to original disciplinary training. Thus, administrators with varying disciplinary backgrounds may have different notions of appropriate standards of evidence for supplied information that are based upon fundamentally different notions of epistemology (Mayo and Kallio, 1983; Mitroff, 1982). For institutional research, these findings suggest that the perceptions of decision makers need to be determined—particularly with respect to the language used—before results are communicated. They also suggest the possibility that different types of individuals can be deliberately induced to play particular informational roles in a group decision-making process (Astin, 1976).

Information Characteristics. Both the content and inherent properties of the information affect utilization. Not surprisingly, simulation studies suggest that results that confirm the preconceptions of decision makers are the most likely to be listened to. In one such study, simulated evaluation findings that agreed with the initial perceptions of administrators were accepted, while those that disagreed with initial perceptions were returned with methodological comments (Eaton, 1956). Not surprisingly, utilization studies emphasize the need for data that are perceived to be of high technical quality (Shapiro, 1986). Furthermore, they suggest that the visual forms in which data are presented can have a considerable impact on credibility (Newman, Brown, and Braskamp, 1980). Summarizing the most frequently encountered technical obstacles to the use of information on student outcomes, Kinnick (1985) notes the excessive bulk of reports, the tendency to organize presentations around discrete data collection efforts rather than around issues or problems, lack of data integrity, lack of face validity, inadequate timeliness, and limited data interpretability. Strategies for overcoming these obstacles in the realm of data communication included graphic presentation, iterative release of information to stimulate a "data dialogue," and redundant data presentation strategies.

Projecting the experience of utilization in program evaluation onto higher education, Shapiro (1986) concludes that the type of information most likely to be used is descriptive and indicative—precisely the sort of data typically generated by institutional research. By concentrating on supplying such data effectively, institutional researchers can ensure a continuing place in decision making. Guided by the experience of evaluation, they can then flexibly and selectively exploit available local opportunities for rendering particular decisions more rational.

References

Adams, C. R. (ed.). *Appraising Information Needs of Decision Makers.* New Directions for Institutional Research, no. 15. San Francisco: Jossey-Bass, 1977.

18

Astin, A. W. *Academic Gamesmanship.* New York: Praeger, 1976.

Baldridge, J. V., and Tierney, M. L. *New Approaches to Management.* San Francisco: Jossey-Bass, 1979.

Braskamp, L. A., and Brown, R. E. *Utilization of Evaluation Information.* New Directions for Program Evaluation, no. 5. San Francisco: Jossey-Bass, 1980.

Brunsson, N. "The Irrationality of Action and Action Rationality: Decisions, Ideologies, and Organizational Actions." *Journal of Management Studies,* 1982, *19* (1), 29–44.

Buhl, L. C., and Lindquist, J. "Academic Improvement Through Action Research." In J. Lindquist (ed.), *Increasing the Use of Institutional Research.* New Directions for Institutional Research, no. 32. San Francisco: Jossey-Bass, 1981.

Campbell, D. T., and Stanley, J. C. *Experimental and Quasi-Experimental Designs for Research.* Chicago: Rand McNally, 1966.

Chaffee, E. E. *Rational Decision Making in Higher Education.* Boulder, Colo.: National Center for Higher Education Management Systems, 1983.

Churchman, C. W. "What Is Information for Policy Making?" In M. Kochen (ed.), *Information for Action: From Knowledge to Wisdom.* New York: Academic Press, 1975.

Eaton, J. "Symbolic and Substantive Evaluation Research." *Administrative Science Quarterly,* 1956, *21,* 53–56.

Ewell, P. T. "Implementing Assessment: Some Organizational Issues." In T. W. Banta (ed.), *Implementing Outcomes Assessment: Promise and Perils.* New Directions for Institutional Research, no. 59. San Francisco: Jossey-Bass, 1988.

Ewell, P. T., and Chaffee, E. E. "Promoting the Effective Use of Information in Decision Making." Paper presented at the 24th annual forum of the Association for Institutional Research, Forth Worth, May 1984.

Feldman, M. S., and March, J. G. "Information in Organizations as Signal and Symbol." *Administrative Science Quarterly,* 1981, *26,* 171–186.

Guba, E. G., and Lincoln, Y. S. *Effective Evaluation: Improving the Usefulness of Evaluation Results Through Responsive and Naturalistic Approaches.* San Francisco: Jossey-Bass, 1981.

Hogan, T. P. "The Wisconsin Evaluation Project." In J. Lindquist (ed.), *Increasing the Use of Institutional Research.* New Directions for Institutional Research, no. 32. San Francisco: Jossey-Bass, 1981.

King, J. A., and Thompson, B. "A Nationwide Survey of Administrators' Perceptions of Evaluation." Paper presented at the annual meeting of the American Educational Research Association, Los Angeles, 1981.

Kinnick, M. "Increasing the Use of Student Outcomes Information." In P. T. Ewell (ed.), *Assessing Educational Outcomes.* New Directions for Institutional Research, no. 47. San Francisco: Jossey-Bass, 1985.

Lazarsfeld, P. F., and Reitz, J. G. *An Introduction to Applied Sociology.* New York: Elsevier, 1975.

Leviton, L. C., and Boruch, R. F. "Contributions of Evaluation to Educational Programs and Policy." *Evaluation Review,* 1983, *7,* 563–598.

McKenney, J. L., and Keen, P.G.W. "How Managers' Minds Work." *Harvard Business Review,* 1974, *52,* 79–90.

Mayo, M., and Kallio, R. E. "Effective Use of Modes in the Decision Process: Theory Grounded in Three Case Studies." *AIR Professional File,* 1983, *15,* unpaged.

Mitroff, I. I. "Secure Versus Insecure Forms of Knowing in University Settings: Two Archetypes of Inquiry." *Journal of Higher Education,* 1982, *53* (6), 640–655.

Newman, D. L., Brown, R. D., and Braskamp, L. A. "Communication Theory and the Utilization of Evaluation." In L. A. Braskamp and R. Brown (eds.), *Utilization of Evaluation Information*. New Directions for Program Evaluation, no. 5. San Francisco: Jossey-Bass, 1980.

Patton, M. Q. *Utilization-Focused Evaluation*. Newbury Park, Calif.: Sage, 1978.

Patton, M. Q., and Associates. "In Search of Impact: An Analysis of the Utilization of Federal Health Evaluation Research." In C. H. Weiss (ed.), *Using Social Science Research in Public Policy Making*. Lexington, Mass.: Heath, 1977.

Raiffa, H. *Decision Analysis*. Reading, Mass.: Addison-Wesley, 1968.

Rich, R. F. "Uses of Social Science Information by Federal Bureaucrats: Knowledge for Understanding Versus Knowledge for Action." In C. H. Weiss (ed.), *Using Social Science Research in Public Policy Making*. Lexington, Mass.: Heath, 1977.

Rich, R. F. *Social Science Information and Public Policy Making*. San Francisco: Jossey-Bass, 1981.

Saupe, J. L. *The Functions of Institutional Research*. Tallahassee, Fla.: Association for Institutional Research, 1981.

Schmidtlein, F. A. "Information Systems and Concepts of Higher Education Governance." In C. R. Adams (ed.), *Appraising Information Needs of Decision Makers*. New Directions for Institutional Research, no. 15. San Francisco: Jossey-Bass, 1977.

Shapiro, J. Z. "Evaluation Research and Educational Decision Making." In J. C. Smart (ed.), *Higher Education: Handbook of Theory and Research*. Vol. 2. New York: Agathon Press, 1986.

Sheehan, B. S. "Reflections on the Effectiveness of Informational Support for Decision Makers." In C. R. Adams (ed.), *Appraising Information Needs of Decision Makers*. New Directions for Institutional Research, no. 15. San Francisco: Jossey-Bass, 1977.

Simon, H. A. *Administrative Behavior*. (2nd ed.) New York: Free Press, 1957.

Smith, N. L., and Chircop, S. "The Weiss-Patton Debate: Illumination of the Fundamental Concepts." *Evaluation Practice*, 1989, *10* (2), 5-13.

Stake, R. E. "The Case Study Method in Social Inquiry." *Educational Researcher*, 1978, *7*, 5-8.

Stufflebeam, D. L. "The Relevance of the CIPP Evaluation Model for Educational Accountability." *Journal of Research and Development in Education*, 1971, *5*, 19-25.

Terrass, S., and Pomrenke, V. "The Institutional Research as Change Agent." In J. Lindquist (ed.), *Increasing the Use of Institutional Research*. New Directions for Institutional Research, no. 32. San Francisco: Jossey-Bass, 1981.

Weiss, C. H. *Evaluation Research*. Englewood Cliffs, N.J.: Prentice-Hall, 1972.

Wilson, R. F. "Program Evaluation in Higher Education." In J. A. Muffo and G. W. McLaughlin (eds.), *A Primer on Institutional Research*. Tallahassee, Fla.: Association for Institutional Research, 1987.

Yavarsky, D. K. *Discrepancy Evaluation: A Practitioner's Guide*. Charlottesville: University of Virginia, 1976.

Peter T. Ewell is a senior associate at the National Center for Higher Education Management Systems (NCHEMS).

Organizational barriers to information use vary with types
of decisions and the phases of information collection, analysis,
and communication. Strategies to overcome one kind of barrier
will not necessarily work for another.

Barriers to Information Use: The Organizational Context

Gerald W. McLaughlin, Josetta S. McLaughlin

There are many barriers within organizations that restrain, distract, limit, and bound the effective use of information. Reducing these barriers requires understanding their context, identifying the problems associated with each, and developing appropriate procedures for dealing with them. This chapter addresses these three requirements by developing and demonstrating a framework within which barriers to information use can be identified and discussed and then by making recommendations for breaking them down.

A Framework for Assessment

In 1971, G. Anthony Gorry and Michael S. Scott Morton developed a framework for management information systems. Most notable was their use of the three levels of managerial activity that Robert Anthony (1965) had identified: strategic planning, managerial control, and operational control. The authors suggested that an understanding of managerial activity "is a prerequisite for effective systems design and implementation" (Gorry and Scott Morton, 1971, p. 7). An understanding of these levels of managerial activity is also helpful in identifying and assessing organizational barriers to effective use of information. Managerial activities will

P. T. Ewell (ed.). *Enhancing Information Use in Decision Making.*
New Directions for Institutional Research, no. 64. San Francisco: Jossey-Bass, Winter 1989.

thus serve as our starting point for identifying constraints on information use. We will then amplify this discussion by applying a second set of information support activities that are typically employed sequentially to assist in information support and organization. The resulting framework is shown in Table 1. Types of managerial activity are represented along the horizontal axis, and information support activities are represented on the vertical axis. Examples of barriers to effective use of information thus occur within each cell. Further defining these dimensions, covering the substance of each cell, and making recommendations to reduce barriers will constitute the core of our discussion.

Types of Managerial Activity

We make two assumptions concerning the types of managerial activity. First, based on a broad definition of information need, it is appropriate to consider managerial activity as processes. This consideration recognizes the fact that, in colleges and universities, these processes occur at all levels within the institution. Second, use of the term *processes* recognizes that the information support function must service ongoing events as well as specific decision-making activities.

Strategic-Level Processes. Strategic-level processes involve identification, development, and focus of overall organizational efforts. They incorporate long-range time perspectives and value relationships related to policy and governance. One distinguishing characteristic of colleges and universities with respect to strategic processes is divergence in goals and cultures within the organization, within its components, or both. For example, the governance process is located in the faculty, while administrative functions are located in a separate component of the institution. Goals of the loosely coupled faculty are linked to standards of their various disciplines, and they may differ substantially from the goals of administrators, who focus primarily on efficiency and organizational survival.

Managerial-Level Processes. Managerial-level processes focus on the allocation and reallocation of resources to achieve some purpose stated within the institution's objectives. They involve mid-range time perspectives and adaptive activities required to adjust to changing situations. Major concerns of colleges and universities in this area often focus on unique aspects of funding and managerial competence. For example, while finances are typically distributed as dictated by an annual budget, frequent revisions based on the availability of funds rather than on the need for funds are not uncommon. With respect to senior administrators, some are in positions because they demonstrate leadership qualities within their profession, not because they demonstrate managerial competence.

Operational-Level Processes. Operational-level processes are the mech-

Table 1. Organizational Barriers to Effective Information Use:
A Framework

Information support activities	Strategic-level processes	Managerial-level processes	Operational-level processes
Types of Managerial Activity			
Selection	Shifting goals	Communication gaps	Inadequate measures
Capture	Governance and policies	Interdepartmental competition	Technology and standards
Manipulation	Inappropriate frame of reference	Mismatch between user needs and analyst	Lack of technical skills and resources
Delivery	Structural rejection	Technology apprehension	Inappropriate timing
Influence	Conflicting purposes	Unethical uses	Powerlessness

anisms that run and monitor the transformation of inputs into outputs. These structured processes involve short-term time perspectives, are based on fairly high certainty, and focus on the implementing of management decisions. Less judgment is exercised because tasks, goals, and resources have already been delineated through managerial-level processes (Gorry and Scott Morton, 1971). Effective implementation of operational-level processes therefore requires a well-defined locus of power at the managerial or strategic levels. Unfortunately, colleges and universities frequently lack this characteristic, which limits their ability to anticipate operational problems. This is complicated by multiple flows of information, the multiple avenues through which decisions can be made, and considerable interaction among individuals who have little regard for a formal authority structure.

In summary, the organizational barriers to effective use of information exist within the context of strategic-, managerial-, and operational-level processes. While such processes establish a context for informational barriers in general, the specific barriers can be more clearly defined by examining relevant information support activities. These activities begin with decisions about the information that is to be collected and end with information-influencing beliefs and behaviors.

Information Support Activities

An effective information strategy requires consideration of and attention to all information management processes. Decisions taken at the very outset when an information strategy is designed automatically have an impact on the success of data utilization. Effective use of information cannot occur where wrong measures are collected or where reliable and valid data are not available (Howard, McLaughlin, and McLaughlin, 1989). Five activities are needed to ensure effective use. All five activities are essential. In fact, these activities tend to be sequential, and the quality of each successive activity depends on the success with which the previous activity was completed. Failure to manage any one of these activities effectively results in imposition of barriers to effective use of information.

Selection: What to Collect Information About. Selection is the choice of an area of interest in which information will be developed and the selection of measures to be codified. It focuses information resources on key questions asked by individuals within the institution or important to the institution, and it is normally guided by the institution's mission, objectives, and strategies. For example, a growth strategy requires selecting information on the institution's environment and on the growth potential of various programs. Different types of information are required for different types of managerial activity.

Capture: How to Collect and Care for Data. Capture is the development and administration of data bases. It includes the coding and storing of data resources. For computerized information, the capture and care of information generally comes under the concepts of data administration (DA) and data base administration (DBA). While all information is not computerized, the primary concepts of DA and DBA apply to computerized and noncomputerized information alike. These concepts determine how to collect and maintain information in a manner that is most consistent with the capabilities of the storage system and the organization's needs.

Manipulation: How to Give Facts Meaning. Manipulation is the conversion of facts so as to enhance or create meaning. It includes the identification of a context, analysis, interpretation, integration, and other similar processes. Manipulation is the step in which data are put into the form that is appropriate for a given user. This definition requires that conversion of the data produce information that the user can interpret and understand and that the data be put into the form that enables it to meet a particular need. Knowledge of the purpose for which the information is to be used and the part of the decision process that it is to support is therefore crucial.

Delivery: How to Present Information to Users. Delivery is the process of providing information to the user or potential user. It includes ensuring that information conveys the message intended by the information support professional to the recipient. In many instances, the first concerns expressed by a user are how to understand information and how the information affects the individual's position. Delivery thus requires the information management professional to be skilled both in enhancing the user's ability to integrate the information provided and in communicating with the user to ensure trust in the information.

Influence: How to Enhance the Value of Information. Influence concerns utilization of the information. The recipient of the information determines what the information is used for and how valuable or powerful it is for specific purposes. Information has power if it reduces uncertainty and helps in managing or controlling the future. If information is neither powerful nor influential, it represents a cost to the institution that produces no benefit. Reasons for failure to use information are numerous, ranging from the apathy of users to feelings of great certainty.

In summary, within each layer of managerial activity, organizational use of information requires five distinct information support activities. All are essential and interrelated. Let us now examine the activities within each intersection so that we can identify some distinct and specific barriers to information use.

Barriers to Effective Use of Information

This section identifies specific types of barriers to information use according to the logic of Figure 1. Each barrier constitutes an intersection between a type of managerial activity and a particular information support activity. The barriers identified here are merely examples. We do not pretend to list or describe all the potential barriers.

Barriers to Selection

Strategic-Level Processes: Shifting Goals. A central theme to guide selection of information may simply be lacking. This frequently exists when a transition is occurring in institutional leadership. For example, new leadership may shift the institution's emphasis from efficiency to the improving of student outcomes, which makes it necessary to select additional data for the measuring of student outcomes. Substantial barriers arise in instances where information support professionals are unable to anticipate these shifts and thus to provide the information needed.

Managerial-Level Processes: Communication Gaps. Basic institutional purposes may not be communicated to those charged with providing information support. Failure to communicate leads to those who select information to ignore the needs and decision processes of the institution. If information support personnel are ill informed, then it is unlikely that others will cooperate in the selecting of information. Problems of selection are further complicated when administrators, faculty, or both erroneously think that they already possess complete information or at least information that is sufficient for the making of a given decision.

Operational-Level Processes: Inadequate Measures. A major barrier to selection occurs when adequate measures concerning the area of interest are lacking. This problem is most noticeable where goals focus on control or growth, both of which rely heavily on environmental scanning for adequate information support (Morrison, Renfro, and Boucher, 1984). Current techniques do not generally permit the integration of environmental scanning information into a manageable and measurable form at the operational level. Unfortunately, when one set of concerns can be measured more easily than another, influence and power tend to shift toward the concerns that have the more manageable data. Relevant information obtained through environmental scanning can thus be ignored.

Barriers to Capture

Strategic-Level Processes: Governance and Policies. Lack of a strong institutional commitment to the information support function can act as a major barrier to effective information use. This problem can manifest itself in two ways: failure to establish a function whose primary responsibility is data administration or placement of the responsibility in a functional area whose primary goal is not related to information support for the overall institution. Furthermore, when no one is responsible for developing policies for the capture and care of data for the entire institution, the authority and resources needed for the function may not be consistent with the information needs.

Managerial-Level Processes: Interdepartmental Competition. Compartmentalization of the institution frequently acts as a barrier to the obtaining of data. One department or functional area simply will not provide the services that another department needs. There may be no advantage to the first party and in some instances there may even be a disadvantage. In other instances, one department may not help another due to inconsistent resource allocation across departments—a situation often exacerbated by cultural factors within the institution.

Operational-Level Processes: Technology and Standards. Three conditions must be present for the information support function to be effective: top-level support for capture of data; technical resources for some type of dictionary and documentation; and guidelines, procedures, and standards that explain how to capture and care for data. Absence of any one condition interferes with information capture at the operational level. A related threat is posed by technology. Noncompatible machines and software within a given institution act as serious barriers for information needed by multiple functional areas.

Barriers to Manipulation

Strategic-Level Processes: Inappropriate Frame of Reference. Lack of agreement among various key groups on the frame of reference in which data should be placed can act as a primary barrier to effective information use. For example, administrators may choose one group of peer institutions for comparative research, while faculty believe that a different group is appropriate. The time perspective of the two groups may also differ. Administrators may rely on trends over the last several years, while faculty substitute criteria arrived at through a paradigm common to their specific discipline. These inconsistencies, coupled with lack of knowledge about causal relationships, interfere with the ability to convert data into a meaningful form.

Managerial-Level Processes: Mismatch Between User Needs and Analyst Perception. Several key roles are inherent in every decision: the person who makes the decision, those who approve the decision, those who are consulted on the decision, those who review the decision, and those who are responsible for its implementation. The information supplied must therefore contain the correct mix of technical detail, managerial implications, and big-picture concepts. Because the individuals who perform these roles are generally at different levels of responsibility, the mix requires qualitative as well as quantitative information. Failure of the analyst to perceive these differences in user needs correctly inhibits the user's ability to interpret and direct implementation.

Operational-Level Processes: Lack of Technical Skills and Resources. The individual working with information may lack the professional skills and technical resources needed in order to manipulate the data. Although there are many analytical procedures (for example, analysis of variance, regression) that may be appropriate for analysis of the data, the information support person may not have the knowledge needed to develop and use appropriate techniques for manipulation of data. In such instances, access to the information that the user needs will be blocked. Unfortunately, the institution may hesitate to commit resources to the training of support personnel in these skills or to the purchase of needed hardware and software.

Barriers to Delivery

Strategic-Level Processes: Structural Rejection. Various core groups within the institution frequently have conflicting goals. Consequently, a major barrier may develop when key individuals have the power to reject information that does not support their position. Rejection can be based on several grounds, including the appropriateness of the measures, the perceived incompetencies of those who provide the information, the presence of an alternative information set, and alternative interpretations of the information provided.

Managerial-Level Processes: Technology Apprehension. Some users either inherently dislike new technology or distrust those who work with it. Some believe that data do not make decisions; others, that great ideas are not based on information. These individuals are suspicious of those who deliver information, they are upset by those who have computer terminals, they do not like computer printout, and they do not like reports with tables that use computer abbreviations. In addition, such individuals are extremely sensitive to the media used to deliver the information. This proclivity for specific types of reports in certain environments must be considered, or the potential value of the information will be lost.

Operational-Level Processes: Inappropriate Timing. Incorrect timing in delivery of information can act as a barrier, because it can cause recipients to ignore the information. For example, the decision may have already been made, or the decision may be so far out in the future that the information is either irrelevant or incapable or arousing interest. This situation arises generally under two conditions: the information source may be blocked and contact with the user impossible, or the user may not have been trained to ask for information with sufficient lead time for the required collection and manipulation of the data to take place.

Barriers to Influence

Strategic-Level Processes: Conflicting Purposes. What supports one user's purposes may distract from another user's purposes. For example, one of the better ways of predicting academic performance is to include race and gender in institutional studies. Unfortunately, some users may perceive use of these variables as legally and morally unacceptable. The sensitivity of these variables substantially curtails their value and use in decision making.

Managerial-Level Processes: Unethical Uses. Charges of unethical behavior are normally based on the claim that information has been screened or manipulated to provide the best or most supportive perspective for the institution. For example, an information support professional who tries to provide information to resolve a conflict between the administrative and faculty or professional cores or outside sources can be viewed as unethical or biased. Questionable behavior can also arise when excessive information is used in an attempt to mask a gap in some decision maker's logic. The most frequent instance of this tactic is when individuals amass voluminous amounts of information, which may or may not be relevant, to counter an external threat to the organization.

Operational-Level Processes: Powerlessness. The information support professional may not be able to provide information that can reduce the uncertainty of information users concerned primarily with operational tactics. In contrast to situations in which information renders the organization powerful due to its potential use as a persuasive weapon or its effectiveness in identifying and managing issues, information may in this case have little power. It is generally unable to prevent, anticipate, or help the individual cope with some event. The information also fails to assist the user in supporting a position politically. Although political support is often believed to be beyond the traditional concept of support at the operational level, the problem becomes evident when the user attempts to implement a plan or direct a project.

In summary, these are only a few of the types of barriers to effective organizational use of information. Just as each information support activity depends on the successful completion of the preceding activities, success in each type of managerial activity is linked to success in the two other types. Solutions to current or potential problems with information should thus be sought within the context of both dimensions simultaneously, and all activities contained in each dimension must be considered.

Recommendations

This section presents some recommendations aimed at reducing the barriers to effective use of information. Three concepts related to the three types of managerial activity will be examined: entrepreneurship activity (strategic-level processes), tactical behavior (managerial-level processes), and bargaining activity (operational-level processes).

Strategic-Level Processes: Entrepreneurship Activity. Barriers associated with strategic-level processes can be reduced by adopting a range of entrepreneurial strategies. This approach, adapted from White (1977), produces general guidelines for coping with strategic-level barriers by developing a viable and relevant information support, institutional research function within the institution.

1. Develop a positive belief about the importance of providing information support. Educate others about the full benefits of your services. Advertise the fact that you are selling a useful service, one that can support the goals of the institution. Otherwise, you may simply end up summarizing and providing numbers for reporting and compliance purposes.

2. Identify viable market gaps for your services. Pinpoint a relevant need for IR support that is not being met by other functions. Voluntarily prototype a product for a specific purpose—for example, a quarterly report for a dean's use—and evaluate the user's reaction.

3. Obtain or develop the best people. People are the key to development of the type of information support service that you plan to provide. Increase skills in critical areas, including communication and interpersonal skills as well as technical skills, through professional development. Reward individuals for their efforts through personal recognition and compensation.

4. Attract resource support and confidence of personnel. Have a credible plan describing what you are going to do. Carefully document the resources that it will require. Gain confidence and support of personnel by demonstrating knowledge of what needs to be accomplished and what has already been accomplished.

5. Achieve market penetration by providing services. Get involved in your institution's information flow by identifying and providing needed support. Leverage your opportunities, and develop loyalties among those who use your services. Develop user groups and faculty advisory groups as ways of penetrating the information support market.

6. Focus your resources and services for mature operations. Once you have become involved in the information support function, think strategically. Remain sensitive to the focus of your institution. Position capabilities for primary information needs, and retain the flexibility needed to provide institutional research support on emerging issues. Network with colleagues within national and regional professional associations to identify potential future needs.

Managerial-Level Processes: Tactical Behavior. While the processes just discussed are excellent ways of positioning the information function to avoid strategic barriers, they must be supplemented with the proper use of tactics. These tactics, adapted from Hart (1974), focus on barriers at the managerial level, although they are applicable in some degree to the other two types of managerial activity.

1. Adjust ends to fit the means. Objectives set during strategic-level processes must be adjusted during managerial-level processes to fit the resources available. For example, system changes impact both the technology and the personnel required to take advantage of it. Prepare the user to expect changes due to technology. Have periodic meetings with individuals who support or use the information system to clarify the services that are feasible for the future and the services that are currently available.

2. Always keep your objective in mind. State the information strategy clearly. Identify a set of functions. For example, providing monitoring information for financial functions, activity information for the academic department, and management study reports for the president. These functions and their related activities become the basic objectives of the information function. If a new project or activity does not fit within the framework, think long and hard about becoming involved.

3. Help the user consider the best information to use. When a user wants to resolve a problem or accomplish some chore, the activity may involve either the offensive or the defensive use of information in a competitive situation. If there are more effective or efficient means for accomplishing objectives, the information support function will be more valuable if it is useful in discovering these means.

4. Exploit the line of least resistance. Investigate the need for services. Identify the services that other functions already provide. Avoid service areas already adequately developed by other functions, since your direct involvement is likely to be seen as a threat to their authority.

5. Pursue activities that accomplish multiple objectives. If one strategy will support multiple needs at a small increase in cost, it may be wise to adopt that strategy. For example, if you desire to estimate student demand for a major while the vice-president of students wants to determine student satisfaction with alternatives and the academic vice-president wants to evaluate satisfaction with faculty advising, a student survey may be best tool for satisfying all these needs. This strategy is heavily dependent on the information support professional's knowledge of user needs, and it can be greatly enhanced by the development user groups.

6. Maintain the flexibility of plans and resources. Rather than work on extensive complicated projects that will tie up resources for long periods of time, try to work with projects that allow the retention of flexibility. Look for existing systems that can be used in implementation rather than tying up considerable internal resources to develop new systems. Focus on prototypes rather than committing resources to untested projects.

7. Do not continue to fight losing battles. If the forces at your institution are predisposed against certain types of information or processes, look for alternatives. For example, if the alumni director does not want to provide addresses of recent graduates, determine whether this information is available from the director of placement. If you cannot survey students in the dormitories directly, use mail surveys. If the president does not like computer printout, use a graphics package.

Operational-Level Processes: Bargaining Activities. Bargaining is the process of give-and-take on specific task requirements relative to time, personnel, and equipment resources. Under conditions of scarce resources and increasing demands, this skill is critical on a day-to-day operating level for informational professionals. These skills are adopted from Keiser (1988).

1. Scan the situation. Identify the potential problems before beginning a specific project. Who wants the information? When is it needed? What specific information is currently available? Try to develop a brief description of the situation that can include answers to these questions and an analysis of the problem.

2. Gain increased knowledge. Find out what others have learned about the topic under consideration. Read several classical articles on the topic, and talk to experts in the field to identify key concepts on which you should focus. Call colleagues at comparable institutions, and see whether they have dealt with similar situations.

3. Develop a general agenda for the project. Aim the agenda at searching for a solution that is mutually beneficial for all concerned. Consider bargaining as a four-step process: excitation (all parties discuss the potential benefits of the information), exploration (alternatives are developed), clarification (the most likely alternatives are focused on), and crystallization (detailed agreement on resources and responsibilities is developed). This agenda begins with the least complicated processes—excitement about new ideas—and moves to the most difficult: the actual assignment of responsibilities.

4. Involve others by asking questions. Move the process from excitation to crystallization by asking questions. Involve other individuals by involving them actively in the search for the best possible solution. Encourage participants to consider the trade-offs between providing A tomorrow and B by next week. Use previously developed questions, such as those developed at the Massachusetts Institute of Technology on critical success factors (Rockart and DeLong, 1988; Rockart and Bullen, 1986) wherever they are available.

5. Balance user services and walkaways. Develop walkaways. That is, determine the point at which you will walk away from a bargaining situation. Accept the fact that there is a point beyond which data are of questionable value due to small samples, unknown causative factors, and so forth. In these situations, the user wants something that the data cannot deliver. At other times, the user may want to use the information in a way that is not consistent with the institution's mission or with your own professional guidelines.

6. Keep notes and documentation. Document all meetings and conversations. The individual who documents can often accomplish more of his or her objectives. Postmeeting memos can help to ensure that issues that have been resolved remain resolved. And, documentation should assist in keeping track of the issues left unresolved.

Summary

Numerous barriers in any organization inhibit the effective use of information. This chapter has focused on a framework that allows institutional researchers to identify and discuss such barriers systematically by examining two dimensions: types of managerial activity and types of information support activities. Development of problems within one type of managerial activity affects decision making processes in the other two types. Similarly, failure to effectively address any one information support activity jeopardizes the integrity of information support in all subsequent activities. Because it is almost certain that such barriers will arise at all levels, information professionals must be prepared to be entrepreneurs, to engage in tactical behavior, and to use bargaining strategies. Professional associations, such as the Association for Institutional Research, are excellent places in which to develop these skills and to learn where, when, and how to use them.

References

Anthony, R. N. *Planning and Control Systems: A Framework for Analysis.* Boston: Division of Research, Harvard Business School, 1965.

Gorry, G. A., and Scott Morton, M. S. "A Framework for Management Information Systems." *Sloan Management Review,* 1971, *13* (1), 55–70.

Hart, B.H.L. *Strategy.* New York: Praeger, 1974.

Howard, R. D., McLaughlin, G. W., and McLaughlin, J. S. "Bridging the Gap Between the Data Base and User in a Distributed Environment." *Cause/Effect,* January 1989, pp. 19–25.

Keiser, T. C. "Negotiating with a Customer You Can't Afford to Lose." *Harvard Business Review,* 1988, *6,* 30–37.

Morrison, J. L., Renfro, W. L., and Boucher, W. I. *Futures Research and the Strategic Planning Process.* ASHE-ERIC Higher Education Report, no. 9. College Station, Tex.: Association for the Study of Higher Education, 1984.

Rockart, J. F., and Bullen, C. V. (eds.). *The Rise of Managerial Computing.* Homewood, Ill.: Dow Jones-Irwin, 1986.

Rockart, J. F., and DeLong, D. W. *Executive Support Systems.* Homewood, Ill.: Dow Jones-Irwin, 1988.

White, R. M. *The Entrepreneur's Manual.* Radnor, Pa.: Chilton, 1977.

Gerald W. McLaughlin is associate director of institutional research and planning analysis at Virginia Polytechnic Institute and State University. In 1988–89, he was president of the Association for Institutional Research.

Josetta S. McLaughlin is a doctoral candidate and instructor in business policy/social issues at Virginia Polytechnic Institute and State University.

Institutional researchers can use cognitive psychology theory and research to improve their support of academic decision makers and to make information more useful and usable.

The Psychological Context: Seven Maxims for Institutional Researchers

Judith Dozier Hackman

Why is it often so difficult for college and university decision makers to understand and use information from institutional researchers? Psychologists have found that inherent cognitive constraints limit the ability of humans to perceive and process information. As institutional researchers, we can learn how to work with, rather than against, these constraints, and we can tap the useful findings of cognitive psychology to improve our information.

This chapter draws on and updates earlier explorations of the application of information processing theory and research to the academic setting (Hackman, 1983). In accord with findings that the span of immediate human memory is limited to about seven bits of information, this chapter examines seven maxims for institutional researchers:

Maxim One: Heuristics are not always helpful.
Maxim Two: Augment humans with models.
Maxim Three: Chunk your data wisely.
Maxim Four: Know your decision makers.
Maxim Five: More may not be better.

P. T. Ewell (ed.). *Enhancing Information Use in Decision Making.*
New Directions for Institutional Research, no. 64. San Francisco: Jossey-Bass, Winter 1989.

Maxim Six: Arrange tables by patterns.
Maxim Seven: Negative evidence and new hypotheses are okay.

Each maxim arises from two basic problems of information processing:
the selection bias inherent in each individual perceiver's decision about
what constitutes relevant information and inherent limits on the number of independent pieces of information that the mind can process
simultaneously.

The discussion of each maxim is organized in three parts: the maxim
is described, essential literature is reviewed, and one or more higher education applications are offered. This chapter does not attempt to summarize the extensive research on information processing but rather to
identify seven guidelines that may be especially useful for institutional
researchers.

Maxim One: Heuristics Are Not Always Helpful

Many decisions that academic leaders must make depend on their
beliefs about the likelihood of uncertain events: which candidate will
make the best dean, what mix of faculty benefits will help retain valued
faculty, which research proposals will be funded, how many students
will be attracted by a new academic program.

Cognitive psychologists have found that humans rely on a limited
number of heuristic principles when they make predictions about uncertainty. We use these simplifying strategies in order to reduce the complex
tasks of assessing probabilities and predicting values. Because of our
cognitive limitations, heuristics are essential and usually quite helpful,
but they sometimes lead to severe and systematic errors (Tversky and
Kahneman, 1974). Three of the most frequently used heuristics, which
also often affect academic decisions, are availability, representativeness,
and anchoring and adjustment (Tversky and Kahneman, 1974, p. 1131).
These authors and others have identified several biases that follow from
these three simplifying strategies.

The term *availability* refers to the availability of instances or scenarios
on which we draw when making decisions. This heuristic is used when
people are asked to assess the frequency of a particular category or the
plausibility of a particular development. Availability biases that affect
decisions include overreliance on the personal instances that the decision
maker can most easily retrieve from his or her most recent, most frequent,
or most vivid experiences. The limitations of the imagination in creating
and considering a set of possible alternatives constitute another kind of
availability bias. The representativeness heuristic comes into play when
people are asked to judge the probability that an object or event belongs
to a category or process. Statisticians and others trained in social science

research methodology should be able to recognize when they begin to fall prey to biases of representativeness; for example, insensitivity to prior probability of outcomes, insensitivity to sample size, misconceptions of chance, insensitivity of predictability, the illusion of validity, and misconceptions of regression. Finally, the term *anchoring and adjustment* refers to adjustment from an anchor, and it is usually employed in a numerical prediction when a relevant value is available. Biases include insufficient adjustments from the anchor value and problems with the assessment of subjective probability distributions.

Academic Decisions and the Availability Heuristic. The use of information in academic decisions frequently trips on the availability heuristic. For example, consider the dean of arts and sciences who is developing a new retirement plan. The goal is to create a policy that will open up tenure positions by encouraging the retirement of less productive faculty while simultaneously retaining the most valued professors as long as possible. One important piece of data is the present rate of faculty retirement at various ages. The availability heuristic may be very helpful in this regard, since instances of frequent events are usually recalled more swiftly and accurately than instances of less common occurrences.

This dean of arts and sciences is a physicist, and at this university the natural scientists and particularly the physicists retire, on the average, three years earlier than faculty in the humanities and the social scientists. Reliance on the availability heuristic may mislead the dean into predicting earlier retirements than are likely. If the dean or his institutional researcher is aware of this bias, then the prediction will be checked against a systematic analysis of the total institution. Unfortunately, we often are not aware of such biases. The five students reviewed yesterday by an admissions committee, the student who caused the most trouble, the department chair who just left the dean's office, the freshman-year experiences of the college president's son—the most retrievable instances are likely to carry the most weight in judgments of uncertainty.

Academic Decisions and the Representativeness Heuristic. Just as a decision maker is likely to call on the most readily available data, he or she also may misinterpret the representativeness of information in predicting uncertain events. Insensitivity to prior probabilities (that is, to base rate frequencies) is one resulting bias. When only base rate data are available, people interpret base rates accurately. For example, the chair of a large biology department knows that for each of the past five years the National Science Office (NSO) has awarded only one in every twenty grant proposals in botanical research. She realizes that the probability of funding for an NSO botany proposal is one in twenty.

Professor Weed is new to the university and has just submitted a large NSO proposal for botanical research. He comes to the biology chair requesting six months of support to get his research project off (or into) the ground while awaiting the decision. If the chair's only information were the base rate, she would surely not gamble on the likelihood of the NSO award. Both earlier research and recent studies of diluting data (Nisbett, Zukier, and Lemley, 1981) suggest that other pieces of data— even irrelevant data—will dilute the accuracy of such decisions. The chair knows very little about Professor Weed's area of research or about the worthiness of his proposal. Weed states that it is ground-breaking research and that he and others in his research group are very excited about the project. The proposal is attractively printed, very thick, and bound in a beautiful blue cover. Extensive charts and graphically pleasing (and expensive) illustrations appear throughout the document. Unless the chair seeks additional information—for example, the base rates for NSO proposals in this area of research with this type of application—she is likely to err in her prediction of the likely outcome and to base the investment of funds on mostly irrelevant data.

Academic Decisions and the Anchoring and Adjustment Heuristic. Difficult estimates of uncertainty often are made possible by adjusting from an initial anchor. This heuristic and its effects are particularly influential in higher education. Examples include the distribution of faculty slots among departments, the allocation of space, and, in particular, annual budgeting. For each of these kinds of decisions, academic administrators naturally rely on anchors from past years or from initial estimates. The author recently became the associate dean responsible for more than six budgetary units in an undergraduate college and offers her personal testimony. She is well aware of the anchoring and adjustment heuristic and the resulting bias of insufficient adjustments. Even with this knowledge, this psychological heuristic and the political context that supports the heuristic make it virtually impossible to implement anything vaguely resembling zero-based budgeting. For example, assume that a unit's ideal budget for next year should objectively be $50,000. If this year's budget is $45,000, the new budget will be lower than it would be if this year's allocation were $55,000, regardless of the unit's objective need for the upcoming year.

The institutional researcher who has internalized the Heuristics Are Not Always Helpful maxim will be alert for the misapplication of the heuristics just described. He or she may even have acquired such an early-warning system by virtue of his or her education. An interesting new finding by Richard Nisbett and colleagues (Lehman, Lempert, and Nisbett, 1988) suggests that people with formal statistical education (for example, most psychologists, doctors and, let us hope, institutional researchers) are likely to be aware of the helpful and counterbalancing heuristics related to statistical rules—for example, "the law of large numbers; the rule that sample values resemble population values as a direct function of sample size and an inverse function of population variability;

and the related regression or base rate principles" (Lehman, Lempert, and Nisbett, 1988, p. 433). In contrast, these researchers found that graduate students in law and chemistry and even psychologists with a natural science emphasis had not acquired the decision-making skills learned from the probabilistic training of social science psychology and medical students. Because of their training, institutional researchers may be particularly good guides around the dangers of heuristics related to decisions about uncertainty.

Maxim Two: Augment Humans with Models

Although models cannot replace human judgment, they can greatly improve certain kinds of decisions. For many higher education questions, it is wise to insert a model at some point in the decision process. We can distinguish between two basic kinds of models: those that directly simulate a phenomenon in question, such as a quantitative faculty flow model or a qualitative notion like Astin's (1985) theory of student involvement, and those that support a decision process, such as the nominal group judgment described by Hammond and Adelman (1976), the Delphi technique, or decision tree. The institutional researcher, supported by the tools of the microcomputer revolution, is often called upon to develop and maintain such models, which can range from simple pencil-and-paper computations to sophisticated computer simulations. Although the term *model* usually refers to the combination of numbers, techniques for combining qualitative data, such as the Delphi technique, can also be so classified.

As Nisbett, Zukier, and Lemley (1981, p. 248) note, "Even expert judges make predictions that are substantially less accurate than those obtained from optimal actuarial formulas employing the same information" (Meehl, 1954; Goldberg, 1968). In fact, expert judges are less accurate than a simple linear equation modeling the judge's own weighting system, and they are even less accurate than equations in which beta weights are randomly assigned (Dawes and Corrigan, 1974). Libby (1981), reviewing research on what he calls *expert measurement and mechanical combination* models, concludes that experienced decision makers are much better at selecting and coding information than at combining and integrating multiple pieces of data.

Academic Decisions and Models. The use of computer models for a limited range of structurable and semistructurable academic decisions has become accepted on most campuses. Both commercial higher education modeling software and campus-grown spreadsheets are regularly used to project the effects of alternative decisions on complicated questions about faculty flow, enrollment size, and budget planning. Algorithms are sometimes created to reflect segments of the admission process, especially in combining multiple test scores, grades, and ratings. On a more routine operational level, most colleges and universities use management information systems to carry out tedious accounting and budget monitoring computations. Monthly budget-to-actual statements are an important augmentation for administrative financial decision making.

The effective institutional researcher will help campus decision makers to identify when and how to use models while ensuring that these creations do not turn into blindly believed black boxes. The finding of Lehman, Lempert, and Nisbett (1988) about the effect of educational discipline on decision making suggests that we may eventually able to help campus decision makers to identify models appropriate to their academic training.

Maxim Three: Chunk Your Data Wisely

The ability and natural tendency of the human mind to organize bits of information into logical chunks or patterns is an essential part of information processing and memory. Our short-term memory for random bits of information is limited to about seven bits (Miller, 1967) such that in a long list of random numbers between I and 1008 we could remember only about seven items (for example, 1, 53, 25, 18, 77, 94, 32). However, if a pattern is discernable, we need only concentrate on one chunk. For example, we could easily remember a list of fifty numbers between 1 and 100 if they were organized by twos (for example, 2, 4, 6, 8, 10, 12, and so on). Another example of chunking can be found in the wording and ordering of the seven maxims in this chapter. (The reader is challenged to discover the pattern used to chunk the seven maxims.)

Maxim three is based on two important cognitive psychology fundings: the span of human short-term memory is limited (Miller, 1967), and people find it difficult to take intercorrelations among information items into account (Slovic and Lichtenstein, 1971). Short-term memory limitations frequency cause decision makers to focus on a subset of the available relevant information. Failure to chunk data wisely may result in less than accurate decisions based on limited but intercorrelated data that give decision makers a false sense of security about their decisions and that may lead them to overconfident judgments (Slovic and Lichtenstein, 1971).

Academic Decisions and Wise Chunking. An example drawn from undergraduate admissions policy illustrates the application of this maxim. If verbal scores from the Scholastic Aptitude Test are highly correlated with English Achievement test scores and if these two test scores correlate in equal amounts with freshman grades, then considering both of the test scores rather than just one adds little to freshman grade prediction. However, the decision maker usually feels intuitively that two test scores are better than one. If Scholastic Aptitude test math scores (which we will pretend for the sake of argument are independent of verbal scores) also predict grades in freshman year, then a combination of Scholastic Aptitude Test math and verbal scores would tell us much more than a combination of Scholastic Aptitude Test verbal scores and English Achievement Test scores. Now, if we expand the number of tests to a list of fifteen scores per applicant to a college, cognitive limitations come into play. Even if there were independently useful information in each of the fifteen tests, which is unlikely, the decision maker will not be able to take advantage of this information in a raw list. In various ways, institutional researchers can prepare and present information so that the chunking process is made easier. In this admissions process example, we might by analysis of past students discover that there are really two chunks of useful information in the fifteen test scores: a mathematical ability chunk and a verbal ability chunk. From knowledge of statistics, we would also know that combining the various mathematical-related scores into one index would give a more reliable measure of math ability than a random score from the set.

At least four applications of this maxim might be tried. First, the admissions committee might know (or we might educate them) that the fifteen scores really measure two kinds of ability, and they might on their own look through the raw data list to identify a student's level on the verbal and math chunks. Second, we might give them all fifteen scores but group the scores visually according to the two abilities. Third, we could group the fifteen scores under their appropriate categories, each headed by a summary index score—one for verbal and one for math. Finally, the admissions staff and institutional research office might agree that it would be preferable to consider only the two indexes without the component test scores.

Maxim Four: Know Your Decision Makers

Awareness and understanding of the decision styles of our academic leaders can lead to more effective information communication by institutional researchers. At a minimum, it is useful to know how decision makers believe they make decisions, including how much information they want, in what forms, and how often.

Recent research by Lehman, Lempert, and Nisbett (1988) about the effects of graduate training on reasoning supports the wisdom of this maxim. Their research findings challenge the twentieth-century rejection by psychologists of "the theory of formal discipline—that is, the view that instruction in abstract rule systems can affect reasoning about everyday life events" (Lehman, Lempert, and Nisbett, 1988, p. 431). Major differences were found among first- and third-year graduate students in psychology, medicine, law, and chemistry on statistical reasoning, methodological reasoning about confounded variables, and reasoning about problems in the logic of the conditional. Both psychology and medical training produced large effects on changes in statistical and methodological reasoning between years one and three. Psychology, medical, and legal training produced differences in the ability to reason about problems in the logic of the conditional. Chemistry training had no effect on any of the types of reasoning studied. The fact that these results can be well understood in terms of the rule systems taught by the various fields indicates not only that the old theory of formal discipline may be at least partially valid but also argues that it is important to understand the effects of decision makers' academic training on their processing of information. More research is, of course, needed if we are to apply these promising findings fully, but they do support the potential importance of maxim four.

Although we should know our decision makers, there is debate about just how extensively information should be tailored for individual members of large organizations, such as colleges and universities (Hackman, 1983). There are at least three arguments against such tailoring. First, Libby (1981) argued that research on information processing demonstrated that the best way of presenting information would be best for everyone, regardless of personal style. (This finding has been challenged by more recent research.) Second, even if there were some best format for a particular decision maker, it is often necessary in large organizations for several people with different styles to use the same sets of information. In addition, the person occupying a particular position may change over time. The wisest path may be to follow what is known about the best general way of presenting information. Nevertheless, we should pay attention to how our most frequent colleagues and our immediate superiors typically process information. It is to our advantage (and their convenience) to understand the preferences of such key people and then either organize information with these preferences in mind or explain why we are presenting information in different ways, given what we know about information processing.

Maxim Five: More May Not Be Better

Most decision makers (and many institutional researchers) believe that if a little information improves a decision, then more information will make it better. Large amounts of data, even if they are not actually used, at a minimum constitute a symbolic homage to rationality. However, in reality more may not be better, and in fact it usually is not. Numerous cognitive psychology experiments demonstrate that the amount of information that people can receive, process, and remember is severely constrained by cognitive limitations, particularly by a limited short-term memory and by the slowness of storage and retrieval in long-term memory (Slovic, 1981). Simon (1957, p. 198) uses the concept of bounded rationality to explain this phenomenon: "The capacity of the human mind for formulating and solving complex problems is very small compared with the size of the problems whose solution is required for objectively rational behavior." Both neurophysiological and linguistic limitations affect our ability to make decisions with perfect rationality.

Even experienced decision makers use much less information than they believe they use. Research with such varied experts as stockbrokers, physicians, court judges, racing touts, and livestock judges has yielded a number of conclusions that can inform the preparation and presentation of information for academic decision makers. First, experts believe that they can make use of large pools of information, but in reality they rely primarily on a few items. Given a list of cues (pieces of information), expert decision makers routinely use less than ten of the items—ranging from two or three cues in studies of judges setting bail (Ebbesen and Konecni, 1975) to six or seven in studies of stockbrokers (Slovic, 1969). Second, the judgment of experts and nonexperts does not improve when the pool of information is increased; indeed, it sometimes is less consistent (Einhorn, 1971). As the amount of information grew from four to six and then to eight items, Anderson (1977) found no increase in multiple correlations with quality of outcome. Finally, expert decision makers seem to use more information is simulated situations than they do in actual situations (Ebbesen and Konecni, 1975; Phelps and Shanteau, 1978).

Academic Decisions and the Amount of Information. What are the implications of this maxim for institutional research? First, we should stop deluding ourselves that more information in a raw form is better and not continue to multiply the amount of data for making decisions. Second, where there is valid information from multiple sources, we can follow maxim two and combine data with models, or we can chunk data as proposed by maxim three. Maxim five has important implications for institutional researchers, both for how we go about preparing and extracting information and for how we then present the information to university decision makers. We should keep in mind that people have great difficulty combining more than six or seven bits of information at a time without some kind of decision aid.

However, in applying this maxim, remember that decision makers almost always incorporate information from sources other than institutional research as they work on a particular decision. Also, because people often think that they do better with more information, institutional researchers will generally be required to produce reams of data anyway. But, when reams are demanded, we can assist decisions by organizing and communicating the data wisely. For example, if the academic vice-president requests everything that you can get for a particular decision, try to find out which things she or he believes are most successful. Together, try to extract priorities for the items of information, and begin work on the top ones. If information low on the list cannot be found or prepared in time, relax in the knowledge that this may be fortunate.

Maxim Six: Arrange Tables by Patterns

When the likely patterns of numerical results are known, tables can be arranged more effectively by making patterns and exceptions obvious. Although there are many ways to apply this maxim, a particularly insightful article by Ehrenberg (1977; see also Libby, 1981) gives four basic guidelines for arranging tables:

1. Round to four significant digits. Rounding facilitates mental arithmetic. More digits may not be better. In more cases, the reader does not need exact numbers, and his or her limited short-term memory does not need to be clogged with extra digits.

2. Use row and column averages or totals. The reader can keep important relationships in mind (such as above and below the average or relative totals among departments) with the assistance of row or column averages or totals. In addition, the reader can compare the table with patterns known beforehand (such as expert chunks from previous years or inflation expectations), and the average and total figures can be scanned for overall patterns and deviations.

3. Present the main pattern of data in columns. When the main pattern of data is organized in columns rather than in rows, the reader can compare individual digits by running the eye up and down a column. For example, a person may want to look for similarities and differences at the thousands level. It is easier to scan up and down the fourth-digit column than it is to jump across the page from left to right.

4. Order the rows and columns by some measure of their size. If the aim is to make comparisons and identify trends, it is useful to order the rows and columns by some measure of size. For example, the largest department may be shown in row one, and the other departments may be organized in descending order of size.

Academic Decisions and the Arrangement of Tables. The information that institutional researchers prepare for decision makers is often presented in statistical or financial tables. Although custom or other requirements may sometimes prohibit the adoption of the four guidelines, it will usually be possible to use all or most. An example follows. The academic vice-president needs to decide whether or not to add a new cognitive psychology faculty position. The psychology chair argues that the major reason why the program has declined in recent years is its loss of funding for faculty, and he requests an incremental full professor position and the requisite financial support. Although the vice-president must consider a variety of quantitative and qualitative information, her one request of the institutional research office is "the financial facts" for instructional costs in psychology for the past six years. She wants to know total salary figures by program for each year beginning with the 1983–84 academic year. We could present the figures in at least two ways. Table 1 represents the old way; Table 2, the new.

Table 1 is drawn from the Psychology Department's annual report, whereas Table 2 applies all four tabular guidelines to emphasize patterns and make the data much more interpretable. The guidelines prescribing rounding to four significant digits and presenting the main pattern in columns will help the vice-president to scan down columns in Table 2 and identify the cognitive psychology "exception." During the past three years, cognitive salaries (and presumably positions) have fallen, while salaries in the other psychology areas have all increased. The guideline prescribing the ordering of rows and columns by some measure of size organizes the programs in decreasing order of expenditure size, which makes it easier to compare cognitive psychology with its neighbors. The guideline prescribing the use of row and column averages or totals provides useful summarizes for comparison. Looking in Table 2 to the left of Cognitive, we discover that in 1983–84 the program was $10,000 behind Developmental salaries, while in 1988–89 the differences had grown to $100,000. Although the overall six-year average of Cognitive is still greater than that of Social, the funds going to social psychology faculty in 1987–88 and 1988–89 are nearly the same. Every program but Cognitive has grown far beyond its six-year average. The 1988–89 Cognitive program is below its six-year salary average.

Maxim six can be useful to institutional researchers virtually every day. When analyzing are presenting numerical information, institutional researchers should remember their own limitations and take advantage of grouping, indexes, and other chunking techniques that facilitate the processing of data. This maxim can greatly ease the decision maker's understanding and use of complex data.

Maxim Seven: Negative Evidence and New Hypotheses Are Okay

The goal of this last maxim is not an indiscriminate search for any kind of data but rather openness to two frequently ignored types of information: new hypotheses and negative evidence. Decision makers (and institutional researchers) who remain open to alternative solutions and disconfirming evidence are likely to make more effective decisions and to avoid early closure on unwise decisions. At first reading, this maxim may

**Table 1. Instructional Costs in Psychology
as Organized in the Department's Annual Report
(in thousands of dollars)**

Program Areas	1983-84	1984-85	1985-86	1986-87	1987-88	1988-89
Clinical	400,813	410,032	422,326	455,677	482,299	510,888
Social	300,083	301,187	306,987	323,562	336,389	350,187
Experimental	240,023	144,401	148,287	159,786	169,483	180,287
Cognitive	340,432	355,924	366,563	367,982	350,000	351,982
Developmental	350,013	361,111	372,199	401,683	425,000	450,483
Total	1,631,364	1,572,655	1,616,362	1,708,690	1,763,171	1,843,827

**Table 2. Instructional Costs in Psychology
Organized by Ehrenberg's Guidelines
(in thousands of dollars)**

Years	Total	Clinical	Developmental	Cognitive	Social	Experimental
1983-84	1,631	401	350	340	300	240
1984-85	1,573	410	361	356	301	144
1985-86	1,616	422	372	367	307	148
1986-87	1,809	456	402	368	324	160
1987-88	1,763	482	425	350	336	169
1988-89	1,844	511	450	352	350	180
Average	1,706	447	393	356	320	174

seem to contradict the prior advice of maxim five that More May Not Be Better, but the emphasis in maxim seven is to remain open only to certain types of additional data. Cognitive research shows that experts begin solving problems by first retrieving a small set of hypotheses from their long-term memory. Starting with available information, these initial hypotheses are based on knowledge about patterns of occurrences that the experts have stored in long-term memory as chunks. The next step is to seek out information relevant to each of the initial hypotheses and to evaluate whether it is confirming, disconfirming, or noncontributory.

Much of the research on expert problem solving has focused on the medical profession. Physicians first generate potential diagnoses from an initial medical workup of a patient, retrieving prototypical symptom patterns from memory. They then test for symptoms associated with each hypothesis. Although disconfirming evidence may cause a doctor to return to the hypothesis-generating stage, Elstein, Shulman, and Sprafka (1978) found in comprehensive investigations that physicians may underweigh or even ignore disconfirming evidence, particularly toward the end of the problem-solving process. Social psychologists have come to similar conclusions about group decision making and offer suggestions aimed at maintaining openness to relevant information. Janis (1972), in his work on groupthink, suggests ways to avoid this trap by appointing an alternating group critic role to group members at different sessions or by inviting visitors to participate. Hackman and Oldham (1979) recommend that groups begin their initial meeting with an active exploration of strategies in order to increase the likelihood that potentially productive alternative ways of approaching the problem will be considered.

Academic Decisions, Negative Evidence, and New Hypotheses. Academic decision makers face complex decisions on a daily basis. What can institutional researchers do to help academic leaders avoid early closure on decisions while not also contributing to the reverse problem of information overload? Awareness that negative evidence and new hypotheses are okay is a first step. Although it may be uncomfortable to enact this maxim, the effective institutional researcher will attempt to maintain openness through such efforts as the preparation of lists of confirming and disconfirming evidence for decision alternatives or the maintenance of an explicit list of accumulating assumptions while working on a problem.

Summary

This chapter has proposed seven maxims in an effort to examine ways in which human information processing theory and research can contribute to the making of better decisions in colleges and universities. These maxims are not meant to summarize the complex and far-reaching work on human information processing. However, the author hopes that she has demonstrated that cognitive research can help institutional researchers in their job of collecting, analyzing, and presenting information to campus decision makers.

References

Anderson, B. L. "Differences in Teacher's Judgment Policies for Varying Numbers of Verbal and Numerical Cues." *Organizational Behavior and Performance,* 1977, *19,* 68-88.

Astin, A. W. *Achieving Educational Excellence.* San Francisco: Jossey-Bass, 1985.

Dawes, R. M., and Corrigan, B. "Linear Models in Decision Making." *Psychological Bulletin,* 1974, *81,* 95-106.

Ebbesen, E., and Konecni, V. "Decision Making and Information Integration in the Courts: The Setting of Bail." *Journal of Personality and Social Psychology,* 1975, *32,* 805-821.

48

Ehrenberg, A.S.C. "Some Rules of Data Presentation." *Statistical Reporter,* 1977, *7*, 305-310.

Einhorn, H. J. "Use of Nonlinear Noncompensatory Models as a Function of Task and Amount of Information." *Organizational Behavior and Performance,* 1971, *6*, 1-27.

Elstein, A. S., Shulman, L. E., and Sprafka, S. A. *Medical Problem Solving: An Analysis of Clinical Reasoning.* Cambridge, Mass.: Harvard University Press, 1978.

Goldberg, C. R. "Simple Models or Simple Process: Some Research on Clinical Judgments." *American Psychologist,* 1968, *23*, 483-496.

Hackman, J. D. "Seven Maxims for Institutional Researchers: Applying Cognitive Theory and Research." *Research in Higher Education,* 1983, *18*, 195-208.

Hackman, J. D., and Oldham, G. R. *Work Redesign.* Reading, Mass.: Addison-Wesley, 1979.

Hammond, K. R., and Adelman, L. "Sciences, Values, and Human Judgment." *Science,* 1976, *194*, 389-396.

Janis, I. L. *Victims of Groupthink: A Psychological Study of Foreign Policy Decisions and Fiascos.* Boston: Houghton Mifflin, 1972.

Lehman, D. R., Lempert, R. O., and Nisbett, R. E. "The Effects of Graduate Training on Reasoning: Formal Discipline and Thinking About Everyday Life Events." *American Psychologist,* 1988, *43*, 431-442.

Libby, R. *Accounting and Human Information Processing: Theory and Applications.* Englewood Cliffs, N.J.: Prentice-Hall, 1981.

Meehl, P. E. *Clinical Versus Statistical Predictor: A Theoretical Analysis and a Review of the Literature.* Minneapolis: University of Minnesota Press, 1954.

Miller, G. "The Magical Number Seven, Plus or Minus Two: Some Limits on Our Capacity for Processing Information." In G. Miller (ed.), *The Psychology of Communications.* New York: Basic Books, 1967.

Nisbett, R. E., Zukier, H., and Lemley, R. E. "The Dilution Effect: Nondiagnostic Information Weakens the Implications of Diagnostic Information." *Cognitive Psychology,* 1981, *13*, 248-277.

Phelps, R. H., and Shanteau, J. "Livestock Judges: How Much Information Can an Expert Use?" *Organizational Behavior and Human Performance,* 1978, *21*, 209-219.

Simon, H. A. *Administrative Behavior.* New York: Macmillan, 1957.

Slovic, P. "Analyzing the Expert Judge: A Descriptive Study of a Stockbroker's Decision Process." *Journal of Applied Psychology,* 1969, *53*, 255-263.

Slovic, P. "Toward Understanding and Improving Decisions." In E. A. Fleishman (ed.), *Human Performance and Productivity.* Hillsdale, N.J.: Erlbaum, 1981.

Slovic, P., and Lichtenstein, S. "Comparison of Bayesian and Regression Approaches to the Study of Information Processing in Judgment." *Organizational Behavior and Human Performance,* 1971, *6*, 649-744.

Tversky, A., and Kahneman, D. "Judgment Under Uncertainty: Heuristics and Biases." *Science,* 1974, *185*, 1124-1131.

Judith Dozier Hackman is associate dean and dean of administrative affairs in Yale College and former director of institutional research for Yale University.

Supporting group decision making requires a knowledge of how groups work, and it can enhance the institutional researcher's role as data supplier and lead methodologist for the group.

Information Support for Group Decision Making

Victor M. H. Borden, Edward L. Delaney

The preceding chapters have centered on the organizational and individual perspectives on information support to decision-making activities. This chapter shifts the focus to the preparation and dissemination of information for group decision support. The conceptual foundation for this topic demands an integration of the individual and organizational perspectives presented earlier and the infusion of a group dynamics perspective as well. These perspectives must then be applied to the actual group decision settings prevalent in higher education administration. Even a cursory introduction to this topic is beyond the scope of this chapter. Its more modest objective is thus to provide insight into ways in which institutional research can be positioned so as to better support group decision-making activities in colleges and universities.

Higher education has always been predisposed to the collegial group decision-making style with its numerous committees, task forces, faculty senates, and governing boards. The prevalence of particular group formats may vary with institutional leadership style. However, it seems clear that strategic, tactical, and operational planning and policy decisions in most organizations, particularly higher education institutions, are becoming more complex and more frequent and that they demand greater participation (DeSanctis and Gallupe, 1987). We think that insti-

P. T. Ewell (ed.). *Enhancing Information Use in Decision Making.*
New Directions for Institutional Research, no. 64. San Francisco: Jossey-Bass, Winter 1989.

tutional researchers will increasingly be challenged to provide information support to group decision makers or be replaced by those who can and will, as Reichard and others (1984) have suggested.

The provision of decision support information to groups encompasses the full range of institutional research functions. For an individual to perform such a role adequately requires sufficient knowledge of the administrative issues confronting decision-making groups, an understanding of decision-making processes among individuals and within groups and organizations, access and analysis of appropriate information in a timely and reliable fashion, and application of information to the process so as to inform and improve decision-making outcomes. After considering each of these requirements, we can address the two central questions of this chapter: what forms of participation facilitate information support to group decision making, and how can one best organize institutional research to respond to the requirements of group decision support?

Knowledge of Administrative Issues

To develop administrative initiatives and the many policies and procedures needed to carry them out, one must have an understanding both of the broad issues and challenges that confront higher education generally and of the form and force that they take at a particular institution. For example, in recent years a shift in emphasis seems to has occurred in higher education administration. This has led many university administrations away from the great enthusiasm for effective and efficient management typical of blue-chip Fortune 500 corporations toward demands for educational reform, improvement of programs and services, and outcomes accountability measures.

The manner in which an institution initiates or responds to such issues depends upon the role and scope of its perceived mission and historical development. As is typical in strategic planning models, an institution's decision to do or not to do things differently is shaped by the demands and opportunities of its environment, the constraints of its resources, and the values held by its leaders. Awareness of the big institutional picture is most commonly held by a select few at the highest levels of the administration.

In contrast, tactical planning and operational decision making requires more intimate knowledge of administrative policies and practice. Consider, for instance, the information requirements of a committee charged with developing plans to reduce staff turnover. Typically, the institutional researcher can at best provide information and methods that help to describe the scope of the problem, for example, trends in vacancy and turnover rates. The institutional researcher is less likely to have at hand or to be able to assemble quickly information that identifies the primary causes and possible solutions to the problem, for example, in-depth exit interviews, analyses of competitive markets, or evaluations of office practices. Information support for group decision making thus requires significant familiarity with both the big picture and the operational detail. Typically, very few in the organization are in a position to provide meaningful insight on the issues and the institution's capacity to change. Thus, there is often a considerable gap between the vision associated with strategic issues and knowledge about their impact on operational services and programs.

But, is the institutional researcher capable of spanning this range? On the one hand, the institutional research function is a somewhat unique boundary-spanning position. This, together with the fact that the institutional researcher tends to be generally knowledgeable about the major issues that the institution confronts and to possess specific information on the structure and content of its various operating areas, often enables the institutional researcher to have the knowledge required for decision support. On the other hand, as Mintzberg (1983) suggests, institutional research appears to occupy a support staff role that is somewhat disconnected from both the strategic apex and the operating core of the organization. While such a role enables the institutional researcher to remain less vested in specific outcomes and thus potentially more objective, it also means that he or she has less thorough knowledge of situational realities and less responsibility for the consequences of change.

A broad knowledge of the higher education and institutional issues should enable the institutional researcher to provide insight and alternative solutions to problems. To ensure that analyses are pertinent and solutions are viable requires continual interaction with those in the organization identifying troublesome issues and those responsible for living with the solutions. Such interaction most typically takes place in groups, formal and informal.

Group Decision-Making Processes and Functions

The study of group decision making has a broad range of conceptual roots. For example, the psychological perspective, as discussed in Chapter Three, focuses on individual barriers to information use. Individual choice, cognitive processes, and interpersonal exchange, which can all be confounded by personal biases and interpersonal influence, are only a few of the basic rational processes of individuals in groups. Out of this perspective comes such helpful advice as Hackman's (1983) seven maxims, which, although intended primarily for the presentation of information to individuals, has equal relevance for group information support. At the same time, the organizational view offered in Chapter One by Ewell and in Chapter Two by the McLaughlins focuses on the constraints that an organization's culture and politics place on behavior. From this view of less than rational process under conditions of uncertainty and incomplete information emerges the importance of multiple, often conflicting, approaches to strategic planning and tactical policy formation.

From another perspective, the literature on group dynamics considers some elements of group conduct that transcend the sum of individual members' dispositions and tendencies. This perspective focuses on the intricacies of group process, which include such matters as group cohesion, communication and information exchange, and task- and social-oriented functions. Additional conceptual frameworks, such as those provided by game theory, and coalition formation offer further insight into the complexity of the group decision-making phenomenon. While the institutional researcher can not hope to master all the relevant literatures, a familiarity with their core concepts is essential for an understanding of the processes that one aspires to support.

There are many functions of group process in decision making. For instance, groups often play a largely social and self-validating function. Arriving at a decision is thus only one of many outcomes of the process. March and Shapira (1982, p. 105) point to the many symbolic and ritualistic functions, going so far as to say that "decision outcomes may often be less significant than the ways in which the process provides meaning in an ambiguous world." Nevertheless, the benefit of group effort is generally acknowledged. Within our own experiences, we can think of instances in which group problem solving was superior to individual efforts. Despite the many frustrations that attend conventional group problem solving, Fox (1987) concluded that several concerned and knowledgeable people are likely to outperform single individuals when solving problems that do not have standard solutions. Furthermore, the superiority of group solutions can generally be attributed to the greater amount of knowledge and information available from the combined membership of the group. But, two other functions of the group stand out with equal importance: the participation of creative key players with significant line responsibilities for implementing the plans that derive from the group process (Dunn, 1984) and the identification of alternative solutions through representation of varying perspectives and information-based discussion (Ewell and Chaffee, 1984).

The success of the process, then, depends not on the presence of a group per se, but on the presence of the right group of sufficiently informed players with differing perspectives on the situation who have the authority needed to arrive at viable solutions. These are the ingredients for the multiple advocacy approach prescribed by Ewell and Chaffee (1984). To support this approach, the information provider must not only obtain both a broad and a specific perspective on the administrative issue of concern to the group but also be able to provide information in support of the multiple managerial styles and perspectives of group members.

Information Access and Analyses

Chapter Two stresses the importance of careful attention to a set of sequential information management processes, particularly to the process of assembling appropriate measures comprised of reliable and valid data. Institutional researchers are becoming increasingly involved in the development of analytic data resources within their organizations. In some instances, the institutional research function is even organizationally housed together with computing and information support functions (Mulhollan, 1988) under the umbrella of a vice-president for information systems or information resource management. If not directly linked to these functions, many institutional research offices nevertheless take on such roles as data administration to ensure the integrity of the information that is derived from the institution's operational applications and data bases. As a result, institutional researchers are improving their ability to derive timely and reliable information from flexibly postured institutional data resources. The ultimate payoff is to spend less time doing research on the data and more on research with the data. As the data resources become more reliable and timely, the institutional research practitioner is likely to spend more time building interactive decision models and other state-of-the-art decision support tools.

But, as McLaughlin and McLaughlin point out in Chapter Two, data that derive from an institution's operational applications alone are very limiting, especially when we consider the information requirements of strategic and even tactical decision-making processes. Such activities often require significant additional information about factors external to the institution, such as national and regional demographics, and normative information from peer institutions. Unfortunately, the availability and the timeliness of external information are often far inferior to the institution's own internal data. Group processes that enable multiple advocacy further require that contrasting sources of information be identified and analyzed. The challenge for the institutional researcher supporting multiple advocacy, then, is to assemble and analyze the most pertinent information obtained from a variety of internal and external sources in the most timely fashion. To keep oneself positioned to perform such a role on a variety of issues with various groups is not a simple task.

Applying Information to the Group Decision-Making Process

The application of information to group decision making has received much attention in the literature of decision sciences. The focus of this attention has been for the most part on the use of information and information technology to structure group process in ways that increase efficiency and effectiveness. Information exchange is at the center of these processes, and the value of information is seen to lie in the capacity that it provides for discriminating among alternatives.

Using Huber's (1982) distinction between nonautomated and automated decision support systems, which that author labeled *dss* and *DSS* respectively, McGrath (1986) distinguished between nonautomated methodologies for the structuring of group decision-making processes (*gdss*) and technology-based methodologies (*GDSS*). DeSanctis and Gallupe (1987) identify three levels of information support for group decision making. Level-one support is geared toward facilitating information exchange among group members. The gdss methods at this level include the use of information as an agenda-setting tool, the handing out of relevant materials prior to meetings, and so on. GDSS technologies at this level include electronic messaging, overhead projectors, computer-driven slide presentations, and other features that are now found in the so-called electronic conference rooms. Level-two support goes beyond exchange, focusing on methods for the reducing of uncertainty in the group process. The gdss methods at this level include the presentation of planning and projection models, such as PERT and Gantt charts, as well as processes for compiling group input, such as the Delphi and nominal-group techniques. GDSS methods automate these processes, enabling immediate feedback on alternative inputs or decision scenarios. Finally, level-three support typically involves machine-induced group interaction (GDSS only), as might be achieved with the automation of a facility that allows for the selection and application of rules to enforce formalized decision procedures, for example, by automating Robert's *Rules of Order*.

It is not likely, and perhaps it is not desirable, that higher education administrators will incorporate such structured level-three methods in the foreseeable future. It is likely that decision groups will begin to take advantage of technologies like electronic conference rooms that enable information to be exchanged more effectively. Again, this will require better coordination of the information that goes into the group process and increased participation and collaboration among information providers. However, nothing can divert the attention of a group away from a difficult issue faster than questionable data provided by a perceived outsider. For most groups, the most legitimate information provider will be recognized when the information provided is perceived to be relevant, timely, and consistent with information obtained from members' own sources or reference group. This is a formidable challenge for the institutional researcher intent on providing information support to group decision making.

Implications for Institutional Research

From the preceding discussion, it should be clear that information support to the broad range of decision-making groups in an organization requires a level of participation that goes beyond the capabilities of a single institutional researcher. How then can decision support information best be provided to college and university administrators as they struggle to make decisions through group interaction?

Deming (1986) advocates that organizations intent on improving quality and productivity should make a leader of statistical methodology a regular participant in any major meeting of president and staff. This position suggests a role consistent with the most widely held definition of the institutional research as one who "provides information which supports institutional planning, policy formation, and decision making" (Saupe, 1981, p. 1). It is interesting to note that such advocacy for major involvement by institutional researchers in strategic planning and policy development has been repeatedly echoed by recent keynote speakers at Association for Institutional Research meetings but that it has yet to be realized at many institutions where institutional researchers are perceived simply as number crunchers and external report producers. However, a growing number of institutions are experimenting with new models.

Centralized Versus Decentralized Models. During the past two decades, some institutions have taken the advice articulated by Deming (1986), perhaps without knowing that they have, and developed institutional research offices staffed by professional analysts from a variety of backgrounds and headed by individuals placed close to the chief executive officers (president or executive vice-presidents for academic or financial affairs). Taylor (1989), who has applied the organizational framework developed by Mintzberg (1983) to the institutional research function, observes that the institutional research function is generally located with the support staff who provide informational reports to external and internal interest groups. Taylor (1989) notes that offices that might more properly be part of Mintzberg's (1983) technostructure are now emerging. The new offices are comprised of those somewhat removed from the operating work flow who enable others to do the work.

While a centralized institutional research office may be able to provide sufficient support to the highest levels of strategic planning, it is unlikely to have sufficient scope to support the tactical decision making that occurs throughout a complex institution. Again, we are faced with the gulf between the big picture and its operational manifestation. However, Saupe (1981, p. 3) points out that "institutional research is carried out in the individual academic and administrative units of the college or university in support of the planning and decision-making responsibilities that reside at the unit level." Although many institutions have a central institutional research office, the research and planning functions are in fact distributed throughout the organization.

Decentralization of the institutional research function may become increasingly prevalent. As Reichard and others (1984, p. 4) observed, "Faced with the retrenchment and financial difficulties in the years ahead, many institutions may discontinue a centralized institutional research function in light of growing capabilities of line managers in generating pertinent and timely management information and analyses." The information age has generated a felt need among unit managers for timely and accurate information that they can use to control their operations. Moreover, information technology is now providing increasingly friendly and inexpensive tools that promote the capture and processing of data. Unfortunately, these expectations and the proliferation of micro-computer-based applications are likely to foster the decentralization of information management, thereby raising the threat of information anarchy and its consequence: group decision making based almost exclusively on intuition and political influence.

To ward off information anarchy, institutional researchers may be increasingly called upon to broker data and definitional differences and ultimately to coordinate the flow of information among decision support analysts. This response may lead to the emergence of institutional researchers as candidates for a new role of top-level information managers—a role that lies somewhere between what has been referred to as chief information officer (CIO) and the lead statistical methodologist described by Deming (1986). From the CIO perspective, this emergent role for institutional researchers is likely to be concerned primarily with broad issues of policy regarding the capture, processing, and dissemination of information throughout the organization. In contrast to the corporate CIO model, the academic role can be somewhat removed from the management of the information resources (hardware, software, and telecommunications) used to process information. However, like Deming's (1986) statistical methodologist role, the CIO function will play a central and key part in determining how information is used in decision support activities throughout the organization. Equipped with a broad knowledge of general and institutional issues and armed with some technical knowledge and skills, this chief information methodologist (CIM) is likely to direct the information technostructure functions envisioned by Mintzberg (1983) as well as the analytical and presentational requirements for the group decision support role.

In any event, even a strong centralized institutional research function will need to increase coordination and interaction among members of the growing cadre of decision support analysts throughout the organization. Such coordination is vital for efforts to improve the links between strategic decision-making arenas and operational areas. In turn, these links help to improve the quality of the data captured at the operational level and to make the data more relevant and more useful for policy and planning decisions. Thus, we think that institutional researchers are well positioned to foster and nurture such links as information brokers among information user groups.

Information Technologies for the Information Broker. Whichever scenario evolves, centralized or decentralized, the institutional research function will be greatly influenced by the challenges and opportunities created by recent advances in information and communications technology. The availability and use of such technologies will require information specialists who can negotiate between information users and the operating areas whose data bases constitute the raw data for management control and strategic decision making.

Several years ago, there was considerable advocacy for the information center model, in which one office facilitates the production of all information, ranging from mailing labels to strategic management reports—even embracing office training in the latest information technologies. Another approach has emphasized the role of the data administrator, whose primary responsibility was seen as one of enhancing the integrity of operational data bases as management information resources. That such efforts have not been widely accepted seems to be related to the evolution of such units from the purely technical data processing and centralized computer center areas. Computer professionals tend to focus myopically on data elements and lack an understanding of the management issues most salient to higher-level administrators and of their informational requirements. Computer professionals also generally lack the analytic skills needed to delineate problematic issues and to suggest actions or viable solutions.

The institutional researcher as information broker may thus be in the best position to enhance the integrity of institutional data bases and the analysis of those data bases for decision support. Who is better able to sort through the definitional issues involved in determining such appropriate measures as student-faculty ratios or meaningful attrition rates? By assuming a greater role in information administration, the institutional researcher of the future is likely to place less emphasis on providing information to others and more emphasis on enabling others to use new and existing technologies to access and analyze information from the institution's corporate data bases. Quality control is typically exerted by making reliable census files with clearly defined formats available to others and by providing appropriate definitions and measures. To do so, the institutional researcher must stay in close contact with both the primary data providers in the operational areas and with evolving information technology tools.

There is also a growing need to supplement and integrate the information from internal data bases with information obtained from external data banks of varying sources. The number of such sources of external information continues to grow. Whether we consider the large-scale peer institutional comparative data sets that can be purchased from the National Center for Education Statistics and other electronic information services or BITNET newsletter electronic dialogues with selected colleagues, institutional researchers must increase their information exchange capabilities. However, while these information brokerage roles are important, they should not be allowed to detract from the capability of the institutional researcher to provide direct methodological assistance—particularly to senior-level administrative groups—as we noted earlier in this chapter.

Summary

In conclusion, this chapter has been intended to induce institutional researchers to recognize the contributions that they can make to group decision making by becoming intermediaries whose main function is to assist groups in structuring their information needs and in facilitating their access to and analysis of appropriate information. This involves an ongoing process in which suggestive indicators are identified, additional questions are raised, the questions are probed by selective in-depth passes through the corporate data base and external information resources, and the process continues until discussion is satisfied and decision is reached. To do so, the institutional researcher should be an active participant in strategic decision-making groups while providing a critical leadership and coordinating role among information analysts throughout the institution. Although the various paths through which the group decision process evolves may be almost limitless, the contribution of an institutional researcher armed with a working knowledge of strategic issues, access to appropriate data, and well-delineated sets of initial indicators will be invaluable to any group decision-making process.

References

Deming, W. E. *Out of the Crisis.* Cambridge, Mass.: M.I.T. Center for Advanced Engineering Study, 1986.

DeSanctis, G., and Gallupe, B. "A Foundation for the Study of Group Decision Support Systems." *Management Science,* 1987, *33* (5), 589–609.

Dunn, J. A., Jr. "Organizational Decision Making." In W. C. Swap and Associates (eds.), *Group Decision Making.* Newbury Park, Calif.: Sage, 1984.

Ewell, P. T., and Chaffee, E. E. "Promoting the Effective Use of Information in Decision Making." Paper presented at the 24th annual forum of the Association for Institutional Research, Forth Worth, May 1984.

Fox, W. M. *Effective Group Problem Solving: How to Broaden Participation, Improve Decision Making, and Increase Commitment to Action.* San Francisco: Jossey-Bass, 1987.

Hackman, J. D. "Seven Maxims for Institutional Researchers: Applying Cognitive Theory and Research." *Research in Higher Education,* 1983, *18* (2), 195–208.

Huber, G. P. "Decision Support Systems: Their Present Nature and Future Applications." In G. R. Ungson and A. N. Braunstein (eds.), *Decision Making: An Interdisciplinary Inquiry.* Boston: Kent, 1982.

McGrath, M. R. "Strategic Decision Making and Group Decision Support Systems." In J. Rohrbaugh and A. T. McCartt (eds.), *Applying Decision Support Systems in Higher Education.* New Directions for Institutional Research, no. 49. San Francisco: Jossey-Bass, 1986.

March, J. G., and Shapira, Z. "Behavioral Decision Theory and Organizational Decision Theory." In G. R. Ungson and A. N. Braunstein (eds.), *Decision Making: An Interdisciplinary Inquiry.* Boston: Kent, 1982.

Mintzberg, H. *Structure in Fives: Designing Effective Organizations.* Englewood Cliffs, N.J.: Prentice-Hall, 1983.

Mulhollan, P. "Information Resource Management." In *Information Technology—Can It All Fit? Proceedings of the Current Issues Forum of the 1988 CAUSE National Conference.* Boulder, Colo.: CAUSE, 1988.

Reichard, D., and others. *Final Report of the Commission to Reassess the Purposes and Objectives of the Association.* Tallahassee, Fla.: Association for Institutional Research, 1984.

Saupe, J. L. *The Functions of Institutional Research.* Tallahassee, Fla.: Association for Institutional Research, 1981.

Taylor, A. L. "Organizational Structure and Institutional Research Role and Function." Paper presented at the 29th annual forum of the Association for Institutional Research, Baltimore, May 1989.

Victor M. H. Borden is management information and research coordinator at George Mason University in Virginia.

Edward L. Delaney is assistant vice-president for planning and research at George Mason University.

Institutional research reports come in many sizes and formats. Regardless of their form, they should always rest on a well-documented research process.

The Institutional Research Report Revisited

Larry G. Jones

Simply put, institutional research reports report institutional research. Masked in the simplicity of that truism are the complexities of the institutions and the phenomena being studied, the research conducted, the findings reported, the use made of the research and reports, and even the manner in which reports are compiled. Given the complex and dynamic nature of the subjects, methods, and purposes of institutional research, it is not surprising that new and different demands are being placed on institutional research reports as well.

In fact, most observers would agree that institutional research reporting has responded in good order to the new demands and expectations of institutional research. However, the concern is not whether this reporting is an appropriate response to changing institutional needs but whether the responses will bode good or ill over time for institutional research and its purposes. Contributing to this concern is the fact that an institutional research report is both an outcome of institutional research and therefore an end in itself and a process, a means to some institutional end.

Clearly, these two attributes of institutional research reports are not mutually exclusive; rather, they are mutually dependent, as in applied research of any origin. Institutional research has value in its own right (as an end in itself) as well as value in reaching some other goal (as the

P. T. Ewell (ed.). *Enhancing Information Use in Decision Making.*
New Directions for Institutional Research, no. 64. San Francisco: Jossey-Bass, Winter 1989.

means to an end). In some measure, how one views the changing form and substance of institutional research reports is determined by how one views institutional research as an end in itself.

Nevertheless, the purpose of this chapter is more practical than philosophical. By discussing some of the pressing circumstances that have influenced the form and substance of institutional research reports, I hope to encourage institutional researchers to take care to ensure that their reports will continue to meet institutional, professional, and scholarly purposes. The intent is not to resolve the conflicts or to argue against organizational and technological change but rather to understand the environment in which institutional research must make its reports. Once the external influences have been identified, it should become easier to find alternative, more productive formats for institutional research reports. The discussion begins with an examination of the purposes served by institutional research reports and the forms that reports have taken. Next, we consider the environmental, organizational, and technical factors that currently seem to have the most influence on institutional research reporting. The concluding section offers some suggestions for keeping institutional research reports responsive to institutional, professional, and scholarly goals.

Institutional Research Reports: A Perspective

Institutional research reports have been used over time to serve at least six clearly identifiable, though not mutually exclusive, purposes: to transmit data; to interpret data; to preserve data; to identify issues; to resolve issues; and to evaluate programs, policies, positions, and decisions. In some cases, the data have been raw—that is, presented as found, without any analysis or manipulation. In other cases, the data have been processed by analysis, manipulation, or statistical techniques. The issues that reports have addressed are often pressing institutional topics, pending institutional concerns or past problems, or broader issues confronting higher education in general. These topics include virtually every conceivable issue facing higher education and a few issues that seem almost inconceivable outside of a particular institutional context. Although institutional research reports have helped to resolve some institutional problems, it is unreasonable to suggest that reports alone have accomplished resolution or that they should be expected to resolve every issue or dilemma. In this case, *resolution* is best interpreted as meaning that institutional research reports have often been used to explore, review, or evaluate solutions or consequences that decision makers might consider. They are often a tool in decision making, but they are usually not the sole determinant of a final resolution. Nevertheless, institutional research reports have been used to present judgmental findings about schools, colleges, departments, programs, degrees, students, faculty, alumni, policies, practices, procedures, and institutional outcomes, most often in the form of an assessment, evaluation, or study.

To serve these purposes, institutional research reports have taken a variety of forms. While some reports have been presented orally, prepared as visual presentations, or transmitted electronically, in almost every case they have also been available in hard copy. Collections can often be found in the institutional research office, in the files of other campus offices, in library archives, or as publications. In some institutional research offices, reports are annotated, and the abstracts are published. In the case of fact books, planning documents, and self-studies, reports are often bound documents published with the intent of providing a permanent reference for the institution.

Some reports have been as short as a single word or sentence; others have run to several volumes. Some have followed a formal research outline and read like theses or dissertations, while others have taken the form of handwritten memos expressed in casual prose or verse. Some reports have been born in crisis and represent ad hoc position papers pieced together under the most demanding of circumstances; others are regularly, routinely, and almost casually produced as published bound documents. Some institutional research reports deal with esoteric topics, whereas others dissect day-to-day, practical issues. The most frequently named varieties of institutional research reports are memos, fact books, position papers, white papers, executive summaries, research reports, institutional studies, projections, planning documents, needs assessments, self-studies, department profiles, fact files, tables, graphs, and figures. The broad spectrum of report types and formats testifies to the responsiveness of institutional research to the wide variety of institutional reporting needs.

Although the personal computer and desktop computer software (or even self-correcting typewriters and good copying machines) have made it considerably easier to produce a sophisticated-looking research report, there is growing concern that some of what is presented as institutional research is not publishable as research. The issue is one not of the importance of what is being reported or of the quality of the research represented but of the style and context in which the data or issues are being presented. Those interested in the publication of institutional research in journals, books, or collective works as a means of presenting scholarly material are often discouraged by what they see in manuscripts. And, researchers who would like to publish their findings as scholarship are frustrated because it is not easy to adjust their work to the traditionally accepted manuscript and research paper format. While this dilemma has been tempered of late, the fact that institutional research reports no longer look like research reports has been lamented not only by journal editors and conference program planners but also by those who fear it may be symptomatic of more serious research deficiencies.

The traditional research paper format is the criterion by which an institutional research report is generally evaluated within the profession. In fact, in the minds of many, the term *institutional research report* is reserved for a report that follows the formal research paper format, which may be why there are so many names for the institutional research reports that do not follow this format. Much of the concern over the evolution of institutional research reporting is based on the observation that new formats for reporting do not follow a standard methodology. Many claim that, not too long ago, the typical institutional research report adhered to the traditional research paper format. If that is no longer true, it may imply important changes in institutional research as a research exercise, changes in how research findings are shared with others, or changes in how institutional research is being used. Conversations with colleagues suggest that changes of all three kinds have in fact taken place. The next section summarizes these conversations and advances an explanation of the factors that have altered institutional research reporting. The experiences of these colleagues probably speak for most of the profession and for most institutions as well.

Factors, Influences, and Forces Shaping Institutional Research Reporting

In general terms, there seem to be three categories of influences shaping the way institutional research reports are written, how they look, and what they are: environmental factors, organizational factors, and technological factors. The specific influences identified in each category have a larger impact on some researchers and institutions than others, but in one form or another they seem to have a universal presence.

Environmental Factors. Time and attitudes shape the form, substance, and context of current institutional research reports. In the minds of active institutional researchers, time is tied to priorities, and priorities are tied to attitudes. Both time and attitudes are considered environmental factors, because they are always present, much like the weather, which everyone talks about but few can change. In contrast, priorities seem to be at the mercy of time and attitudes. In discussions with colleagues, time was mentioned most often as determining the character of institutional research, and it was often linked with organizational and technological influences.

These accounts suggest that institutional researchers have shorter hours, days, weeks, and months than the average person. One can hardly find institutional researchers or institutional research offices that have the time needed to complete any project in the manner that they would choose. Time is the one resource that even the best personal or institutional budget cannot provide in a quantity or quality sufficient to satisfy anyone. Yet, time is also the resource that individuals think someone else has in abundant supply.

Even with the best research and planning, the researcher or the requester can anticipate only a small portion of institutional research requests, and the requests are seldom without some element of urgency. Research and reports that can be anticipated or that come with realistic time frames for completion are most often set aside in favor of more immediate and pressing concerns. Simply put, as the requests for institutional research reports increase, the time frames for completion are shrinking. Moreover, it is not just the researcher who faces the time bind. The people who request the institutional research reports are asking for executive summaries, one-page reports, or figures and tables, not long explanations or interpretations. They explain that they have no time to read a complete report. The emphasis is on the bottom line or the lower right-hand corner. Few researchers have time to write the complete report, and fewer still have time to write a report that will not be read because of its length. Quick and dirty may not be preferred, but it is pervasive.

Among the various solutions for the time problem, shortening the institutional research report seems to have been generally accepted. Busy administrators who thought they could buy time by adding associates and assistants have increased the time demands on institutional research offices by doing so and, many suspect, increased their own time demands as well. Computers have made some tasks quicker and easier, but they have also added to the tasks that can and should be done: the time that computers have saved has then been spent doing additional things. Similarly, personnel added to institutional research offices have quickly had their time consumed by increased requests. The short report, which ironically may not be less time-consuming to produce, has evolved to occupy a position of major importance in institutional research reporting.

Attitudes. In part, the short report reflects increasingly prevalent public and academic attitudes that find research reports stuffy and boring, that focus on the bottom line or lower right-hand corner, and that favor the superficial over the substantive. These attitudes are often held by researchers as well as by readers. While it may not be appropriate to term the academic community anti-intellectual, some of the attitudes that colleagues mentioned as influences on institutional research reports can be viewed as such. At the same time, such pressures are in large measure a reflection of positive attitudes toward institutional research, toward the necessity for informed decisions, and toward the need for evaluation, analysis, and interpretation. Nonetheless, even the most positive attitude toward institutional research may not be supportive of the formal institutional research report. The attitude determining the preferred form and substance of a report is likely to be set by time constraints and attitudes linked to organizational and technological factors.

Organizational Factors. In a sense, the organizational factors that have influenced institutional research reporting reflect attitudinal or philosophical changes in college and university administration. This section examines seven categories of organizational influence. Of course, the categories are interrelated, and they are probably not as discrete as the discussion suggests. In some cases, one might argue that the organizational changes are indicative of a problem for the institution, not for institutional research reporting, or that the influences are external to the organization. Both positions may be true, but the institution and institutional research must respond in appropriate fashion.

Quantitative Management. One does not need to resolve the question of whether the quantitative management movement preceded the general availability of data or vice versa to recognize that college and university management is now data intensive (though not necessarily data managed). When data were hard to come by, decisions were based on a few key data elements. As data became more accessible and available, the data studied and used in management and decision making increased. More data required more analysis, and more analysis required more data. At many colleges and universities, institutional research offices were created to provide data and data analysis so that administrators would be free to make decisions. The need for institutional research reports became firmly established: very often the people who collect and use their own data do not write reports about it. Many argue too, that the requests for data increased when someone else had to do the collecting and reporting.

New Administrative Managers. Although it would be hard to show cause and effect, some of my informants suggested that the increase in data accompanied an increase in the need for managers capable of dealing with the data. In any event, colleges and universities seem to have increased the number of managers, assistants, and assistant and associate deans or vice-presidents or the percentage of directors, department, and division heads whose needs required institutional research reports. These users have changed the nature, quantity, and quality of the data collected, analyzed, and reported. "We are studying more and more about less and less," one researcher said. As the unit of analysis gets smaller (divisions, departments, degree majors, courses), the number, form, and substance of the report change.

Sophisticated Data Users. Along with this perceived increase in the number of people using information is a consensus among institutional researchers that the users are becoming more sophisticated both about the information and about the analyses that they request. Many are asking for second- and third-level data analysis (regressions and ANOVAs, not just counts and averages), more sophisticated models, and more substantial statistical techniques. And, larger numbers are reported to prefer doing their own data analysis. Interestingly, increases in data collection and analysis by others on campus have apparently heightened, not lessened, institutional research activity. Now, institutional research has to verify the reports of other offices or, by mutual consent or decree, provide the "objective" data and analysis needed to drive or reconcile them. New data users are bringing with them the research and reporting expectations of a wide variety of disciplines, perspectives that have not always been represented in institutional research or administration. The new form and substance of institutional research reports is in part a reflection of these new backgrounds.

Institutional Research Involvement in Administration. On many campuses, there has been an organizational evolution for institutional research as well. Once functionally located outside the administrative or decision-making process and reporting in, institutional research offices are now more often represented on administrative "cabinets" or "councils" and meeting directly with committees to give status reports and expert opinions. Presenting a report in person, most suggest, is different from reporting in absentia. As institutional research has moved into the inner circle of administration, the profession has openly debated the question of whether institutional researchers should make administrative policy decisions. Most institutional researchers feel that they are now more centrally involved in institutional decision making than they were in the past, and most feel that this involvement has influenced the issues they consider as well as the form and substance of their reports.

Interest in External Data. The new style of management and the new breed of data users have an increasing interest in data generated outside the institution. In addition to the environment-scanning sort of reporting, they request increasingly normative and comparable data on peer institutions. Dealing with internal data is hard enough, but, as most institutional researchers have discovered, dealing with data from other institutions—even when definitions have been mutually set—demands even more reporting skill. National data bases can be problems in their own right, and dealing with analyses based on those data by other campus users can be particularly troublesome.

New Interrogators. At the same time that colleges and universities are turning their attention to external data, the institutions themselves are becoming the focal point of external examination. It is one thing to share data with other colleges and universities but quite another to respond to legislators, coordinating boards, state commissions, and the federal government, not to mention other constituencies who feel they have a need or right to know. Reports to off-campus groups, many of which are not versed in academic terminology or definitions, are a growing problem for institutions. In many cases, such groups are looking for answers to their questions in their own formats, regardless of whether the questions or the answers will in fact tell them what they want to know. Some sense that the new data and research agenda for institutions is being set by off-campus users, who are dictating on-campus as well as off-campus reporting form and substance. Those holding that attitude approach institutional research reporting in a different fashion from those who believe otherwise.

State Sunshine Laws. Potentially the most troublesome of all influences on institutional research reporting are the state sunshine laws: legislation that gives the public access to virtually all data and reports at public institutions. Early rulings on sunshine cases have generally not provided protection to reports and data originally thought to be confidential, and, to avoid being forced at a later point to release information that might be misinterpreted or misused, some researchers are refusing to analyze or report data unless it is requested that they do. Others are limiting their reporting to specifics and taking extra precautions to maintain the integrity of data sources and files. This growing attitude that all records and reports are public information is supported by legal precedent, and it has the potential to revolutionize institutional research reporting.

Technological Developments. Closely related to the organizational factors that influence institutional research reporting are some technological developments that have accelerated, if not created, reporting techniques, formats, and substance. Again, although the categories are arbitrary, they reflect the distinctions that colleagues make among the several influences.

Accessibility of Data. The form and substance of institutional research reporting has altered with each step in the evolutionary process of data accessibility: from the time when data were collected by hand from files or hard copy documents; to the period when data were taken from punch cards and later from computer cards (often after significant programming effort); to the era of data maintenance on computer tape or disk and extraction by SPSS, SAS, or some other statistical or reporting software; to today, when data can be downloaded or entered and stored on microcomputers and analyzed by spreadsheet. Early reports often demanded major research efforts just to obtain the data, and describing how the data were obtained was therefore an important part of the report. Later reports often consisted of summaries of mountains of computer printouts, which were the result of programming that could never seem to present the data in exactly the right way. Now, of course, the data can be manipulated and reported in a finished form that was unthinkable five years ago. No one disputes the fact that institutional research reporting has progressed quantitatively and qualitatively in direct relation to the accessibility of data.

Availability of Data. The other side of data accessibility is data availability: being able to use the information once it has been obtained. As the data became more accessible, they also became generally more available. In the past, the data were available only to the person who had the file; later, only to those who had access to the system hardware, software, or both. Now, data are often available to anyone with an account number, a need to know, or a microcomputer. The evolution in institutional research reporting maintained a direct relationship to data availability.

Data Manipulation. Perhaps even more important to institutional researchers, for whom data accessibility and data availability posed no serious problems, were the technological developments that made data easier to manipulate. Hand tabulations, calculator statistical computations, and later FORTRAN and COBOL programming tools are reported to have discouraged institutional research in the past that is now considered rather routine. Packaged software like SPSS and SAS made data analysis and reporting much easier but not so easy as it has recently become with microcomputers and spreadsheet software. New form and substance are possible in institutional research reports created on microcomputers, and some old reports have taken on a new life with the latest machines and software.

Data Presentation. Desktop publishing software may provide the most visible influence on institutional research reporting. A visually attractive report will at least be looked at, and it is becoming much easier to produce fancy reports. Just getting tables typed on a ditto master or stencil was once a major task (correcting an error seemed to take a miracle); self-correcting typewriters and Xerox machines were considered revolutionary. Now, four-color figures, three-dimensional graphs, and reports with several type fonts in different sizes—plus boldface and italics for extra measure—are commonplace. Even if institutional research reports are saying the same old thing, they no longer have to look like the same old documents. Many claim that when you can present data is a more attractive way, you often find more attractive data to present. Electronic mail is another technological development that has potential for influencing institutional research and reporting, particularly in the collection and delivery of data.

Conclusion

Documenting the changes that have influenced the form and substance of institutional research reports is not difficult. Tangible evidence of those influences can be found in the reports of every institutional researcher. It would be foolish to argue that the evolution, adaptation, or outright alteration of institutional research reports in response to changing institutional needs has been less than appropriate. In fact, researchers should be commended for making the most of the new technologies and opportunities in their reporting and for being leaders in the process. But, there appears to be no universal reporting response to these influences. Not all researchers have responded in the same fashion to the same influences, nor have they necessarily responded in the same way twice. Institutional reporting is clearly situational. Moreover, the form and substance of the report are dictated by any number of factors and only rarely by any prescribed form or method of reporting.

Obviously, the traditional, formal institutional research report is less likely to be the model for institutional research reporting than it may once have been. Nevertheless, it is still considered by many to be the standard against which institutional reports should be judged. Some lament the passage of this kind of report, perhaps because of its form, but more express concern over the demise of the research discipline or process that it represented. It would be disastrous for many reasons if the traditional institutional research report were to disappear completely. It has yet to do so. While the quantity may be down, the quality is reported to be at least stable if not better. However, there will be serious consequences if the basic research processes so well represented by the format of the traditional, formal research report do not remain as the basic outline for all institutional research. Regardless of the form that a report takes, the research itself must address in some fashion the traditional report's ingredients: statement of the problem, review of the literature, appropriate data, appropriate methodology for data analysis, report of findings, and consideration of additional study. While it is possible to write a research report without all the component parts of a formal research study, it is impossible to have anything to report unless consideration continues to be given to each part.

If proper attention has been given to the research process, the way in which the findings are reported is either immaterial or subject to other considerations. According to practitioners, a good institutional research report starts by following appropriate research methodology. With that as a given, the good report is obliged to meet just four basic criteria: it must answer the question with the best available data, it must call attention to any necessary research caveats, it must follow a format acceptable to the user, and it must be completed in a timely fashion. How these criteria are met is left to the individual and the institution.

In a perfect world, one type of report would serve all institutional and scholarly purposes. In the real world, a formal research report that meets scholarly purposes does not meet the practical needs of an institution, and the formats that meet institutional needs do not serve the scholarly community. Fortunately, there is a report format to meet every purpose. The basic problem for the institutional researcher is only to find the right one.

*Larry G. Jones is associate director of institutional research
at the University of Georgia.*

Usable partial data available at the right time are far more
valuable than perfect data a month later. New technologies are
making this elusive goal ever more attainable.

Electronic Media and Information Sharing

John A. Dunn, Jr.

Information made available through electronic media is beginning to impact institutional decision making. Consider the following examples: The provost of a midwestern liberal arts college is concerned about a drop in the number of applications at an early point in the admissions cycle. With a single query to an electronic discussion list that reaches more than fifty similar institutions, he or she learns in a few days that most have experienced the same decline and to about the same degree. A major public institution posts all proposed faculty and staff policies on its electronic mail system for comment, getting responses from both expected and unexpected quarters. Readers of an electronic newsletter published for a higher education association learn that a major state university system is reviewing existing guidelines on use of space, and more than thirty request copies of the proposed new version. A state higher education coordinating board circulates all proposals and receives responses to them electronically, speeding the process and avoiding any "lost in the mail"

I want to express gratitude to Mark Meredith of the University of Colorado, John Muffo of Virginia Polytechnic Institute and State University, and Daniel A. Updegrove of EDUCOM as well as to volume editor Peter Ewell for comments and suggestions helpful in the preparation of this chapter.

P. T. Ewell (ed.). *Enhancing Information Use in Decision Making.*
New Directions for Institutional Research, no. 64. San Francisco: Jossey-Bass, Winter 1989.

73

excuses. Members of a data-sharing consortium forward their question-naire responses to a central office and receive the comparable information for all participants in return in both paper and diskette format. They can then select the fifteen or twenty institutions that they regard as peers, erase or move the uninteresting data, and create instant comparative studies. Members of another set of major research universities share an electronic bulletin board. Anyone can open a topic; all others are invited to read and respond. Over the course of a few days, a substantial multiparty dialogue will have been recorded, perhaps on a subject like faculty replacement planning, and all participants can have the benefit. At one university, an on-line fact book provides a variety of confidential data, and access is restricted to senior administrators. At another, the entire fact book is made available to everyone on campus who has access to a terminal; only a few printed copies are produced for archival purposes.

These examples show how electronic media can be used to make information for decision making far more accessible than it has ever been. While it may be difficult to trace the precise effect that the provi-sion of broader and more timely information has had on specific institu-tional decisions, it is at least clear that such information provides a better context for decision making.

Definitions

In order to focus this discussion, I will restrict the topic to the effects of electronic media in enhancing access to information, ignoring other electronic manipulation of information. With this definition, it is appro-priate to talk about facsimile (so-called FAX) transmissions; about elec-tronic mail, newsletters, bulletin boards, and discussion lists; about electronic access to data bases far and near; and about electronic data-sharing arrangements. These media are beginning to provide a revolution on campus as liberating as the personal computer revolution. The per-sonal computer freed the individual from dependence on a central data processing operation for access to data and services and extended the individual's abilities. Electronic communications media liberate the indi-vidual from dependence on intermediaries and printed materials in seek-ing information and thereby extend the range of the individual's contacts far beyond the borders of the campus.

I exclude from discussion here the wide range of interesting and pow-erful (and equally electronic) applications in the management and manip-ulation of data—for example, data analysis with SPSS, SAS, or similar tools; the arraying of data with data base management tools; modeling and projecting using spreadsheets or other tools; integration of these packages into decision support systems or expert systems; and the presen-tation of information that uses these and document preparation packages.

These are all valid and productive ways of managing data once the data are in hand, but this chapter will focus on finding and transmitting the data rather than on managing them.

Daniel Updegrove (1989b, p. 2) defines these technologies as follows:

Electronic mail is a computer-based system for exchange of textual messages and other computer files, which may contain numeric or other character-formatted data, computer programs, documents, and (in some advanced systems) binary-formatted data, including graphics. "E-mail" is one of the most common applications of time-shared computers, wide area computer networks, and (more recently) local area networks because it addresses a widespread need for rapid, easy, inexpensive communication with individuals and groups, all of whom need not be available simultaneously (as in telephone conference calls). Electronic mail should be distinguished from two related forms of electronic communication, voice mail and fax. Voice mail is a computer-based system for exchanging voice messages, which can be recorded, reviewed, forwarded, filed, and retrieved from local as well as remote telephones; such systems are especially popular among nontypists and those who travel frequently. Fax is a system for transmitting images via telephone lines; the typical fax machine is a dedicated device containing a scanner for converting printed images into digital form, a modem for sending and receiving the data, and a printer. Faxes are extremely easy to use and have the advantage over most e-mail systems of transmitting graphics as well as text; unlike e-mail, however, the transmission is not easily input into a computer, because most fax machines lack optical character recognition software. Although it is useful to keep these three technologies distinct conceptually, there are in fact merging. For example, the computer workstation introduced last year by NeXT, Inc. features voice mail integrated with electronic mail, and several companies have recently announced software for sending and receiving faxes on personal computers.

Electronic mail can be used in a variety of ways:

Electronic mail's simplest form is one person's sending a message to another. To circulate news or questions to a pre-established audience (for example, chapter authors writing an edited book, board members of an association, or subscribers to a common-interest list), an electronic mailing list can be used. Such a list can be set up with a variety of options, such as open self-subscription versus subscription controlled by a designated individual, or messages only from the list manager versus messages from any subscriber. Lists may be used to distribute electronic newsletters, or to support wide communication among the group, or both. Some mailing list software (for example, LISTSERV) can archive the message traffic, but most message traffic is ephemeral, and saving useful messages is up to the recipient. Electronic conferencing or "bulletin-board" software (for example, CONFER) was developed to support sharing of information on topics of mutual interest by accumulating related messages. A manager sets up a topic, and any member of the subscriber group can contribute to the discussion and can read all contributions to date [Updegrove, 1989b, p. 2].

There are a variety of electronic networks. Much of the discussion here will center on BITNET, the general-purpose network used by a great many colleges and universities.

It will be obvious that many of the tools discussed in this chapter are simply electronic versions of standard institutional research activities or products. Person-to-person electronic mail replaces telephone calls or memos. Inquiries to electronic discussion lists often simply replace (or, in a transitional stage, supplement) paper or telephone surveys. On-line fact books supplant or complement printed fact books. The electronically edited and delivered research report may reach more people, but it is essentially not different from its paper counterpart. The electronic media have the advantages of speed and breadth associated with the communication network. They supplement but do not replace the careful statistical analysis and thoughtful interpretation of the traditional institutional research report.

Information for Institutional Decisions

In what ways can information provided through electronic media be helpful in institutional decision making? To answer this question, we need to consider the nature of administrative decision making.

Herbert Simon (1961) pointed out that most decision makers "satisfice" rather than optimize. Unlike the decision maker in economic theory who always has perfect information and who pursues a single goal, such as maximization of profits, administrators pursue many goals simultaneously—for example, maintaining academic quality and avoiding antagonizing the faculty while raising tuitions but not increasing salaries—and they have to make decisions with the best information that can be obtained at the time. Decisions are not simply emotional or whimsical; they are based on information, but they are necessarily based on incomplete and imperfect information. They are rational, but their rationality includes values, anecdotes, the mythology of the institution, consideration about impacts on others, and considerations about the process of implementing the decision to be made.

Although administrative decisions can be made by a single individual, they are usually to some degree group decisions. The responsible individual depends on his or her colleagues for the information on which the decision is made and for implementing the decision intelligently and willingly. The responsible individual is therefore limited in the options available. The "right" decision among a group of more or less satisfactory alternatives will be the one that the group will support (Dunn, 1984). Whether the group decision dynamics are structured in the multiple advocacy mode suggested by Ewell and Chaffee (1984) or more traditionally, it is important for all involved to have the same information, to have it in time, and to be able to work with it on their own. The electronic media can help by speeding the information dissemination process, by helping each person to gather relevant data, and by aiding in the interpretation, management, and presentation of the information.

In any institution, there is a very wide range of decisions to be taken. Decisions differ sharply in the degree to which they can be anticipated; in their strategic, tactical, or operational character; in their urgency; and in the kinds of inputs that are relevant to the decision process. Institutional budget decisions tend to be made each year at the same time and to follow an elaborate cyclical pattern. The experienced researcher can generally anticipate and gather in advance the information that is likely to be needed. Electronically provided data, such as comparative studies of areas of cost, may be of value here, but time usually permits paper surveys as needed. However, other decisions can be made at any time of the year, and they can be ad hoc; these are hard to prepare for. Examples include a revision in a personnel policy, a change in reporting relationship, and the need to respond to a new demand from the host community. The researcher may well receive a request for peer-group data to be provided in time for a meeting of senior administrators on the following day or for a community meeting in two days' time. Questions can be highly specific (for example, what do schools pay for fire services?), or they can be very unstructured (for example, how are schools like us dealing with their communities?). Here, the ability to query a number of institutions by electronic mail individually or through a discussion list is particularly valuable.

As the McLaughlins emphasize in Chapter Two, the decisions to be made can be operational, tactical, or strategic. The registrar may want to change the room-scheduling paradigm and request some help in finding out what the experience of others has been with a block schedule. Here, a bulletin board application or a broad query of a discussion list might be helpful, since the registrar may not know which other institutions operate on a block schedule. The provost may seek the best tactical approach for dealing with the new federal ruling abolishing mandatory retirement at a certain age (effective at the end of 1993). A query to institutions similar to yours might produce within days answers to such questions as these: Have you eliminated mandatory retirement policies for faculty? for staff? If so, when was the action effective? If your policy has not changed, are you currently considering such action? If your mandatory retirement policy is still in force, are you making exceptions? Answers from a group of institutions may help to suggest how the issue can be dealt with at present and over the next few years. Strategic questions are the most difficult to provide information for, since they are infrequent and unstructured and since they often rely as much on values, intuition, and leadership as they do on factual data. Examples of such decisions are significant changes in pricing strategy, the starting or stopping of major programs, and the undertaking of major construction projects of capital campaigns. Nonetheless, data on how your institution is doing vis-à-vis its peers, early reports on events and trends on other campuses, and similar bits of information may turn out to be significant.

While it sometimes happens that an administrator comes to a situation cold, studies all the data presented in a systematic way, and renders an instant decision, that does not tend to be the rule. Even an instant decision is based to some extent on some previously formed (if not explicitly articulated) set of values or guidelines. The new information is not what really makes the decision; the fit does. Most decisions tend to evolve, if only within the mind of the decision maker. By the time a public decision is needed, key players have long since recognized the need for a decision, formed opinions, expressed their views, and discussed alternatives. The most important use of information at the decision stage may be to convince others. In such cases, the ability of the electronic media to support discussions among key administrators, to facilitate the gathering of peer comparisons, and perhaps even to expose drafts of possible decisions to selected audiences can be helpful both in shaping the decision and in selling it.

Finally, it is clear that different decisions require very different kinds of inputs. For some, factual information drawn from inside or outside the institution provides the key. For others, political considerations of the effects on faculty, or staff, or students, or external supporters may be critical. For instance, an economically sound scaling back of a tuition remission benefit may be dropped if there is the prospect of a faculty upheaval. Peer data can be particularly important in any of these situations. Comparisons may be invidious, but they can provide an orientation to the market, tips on where things are leading, and a comfort level if you propose doing the same things that others are doing. It is important to take advantage of other people's experience—to find out what works, to avoid reinventing the wheel, to be tipped off to considerations that you had not yet thought of, and to see the effects of a possible policy as applied elsewhere.

It should by now be clear that several common threads run through this analysis of decision types. To summarize: the advantages of the electronic media include speed of response and the breadth of the communication network, but they also include the introduction into the decision-making process of information from beyond the campus walls and the provision of qualitative and anecdotal as well as numerical information. These are major advantages.

Advantages of the Electronic Communications Media

When you try to persuade a senior administrator that your college should join an electronic network, you may find that some of the benefits that are easiest to explain offer only marginal advantages. Communicating with someone by electronic mail is easily understood as being much like communicating by telephone but offers the advantage of "time shifting" and thereby eliminates telephone tag. You send a message on your time. The addressee returns it on her time. You can keep electronic record as a log of the communication. The administrator may reply that telephones are still useful for most purposes and that fax transmissions should speed communication and provide written records at far less cost than an institutional hookup.

Networked electronic communication is not free. For instance, an institution linked to BITNET pays for a leased line to the nearest other attached user and for necessary software, a network fee, and some machine time. Typically, BITNET members do not impose per-message charges, although some may allocate the fixed charges among users. Access to other networks may be through dial-up connections, which keep fixed charges low but impose a per-use fee. If the only benefits of networked electronic communication were speed and recordkeeping, these costs might well offset them. Other ways of using electronic communication are harder to explain to those who lack direct experience with it, but they are more cost-effective: for example, several administrators or faculty members may be developing a policy, or a questionnaire, or an article, passing it back and forth, each editing and forwarding it; the added speed and facility of e-mail communication supports such collaboration in ways that other, slower forms of communication simply cannot. The fact that there is usually no per-unit cost for each message means that colleagues can be in more frequent and therefore more productive contact. Receiving text or data in machine-readable form greatly facilitates the researcher's task of making use of the information. The ability to edit documents, to extract from reports, and to array and analyze data, all without having to rekey them, saves substantial time and effort. However, the most important breakthrough comes when one person has the ability to communicate with many, either by sending out newsletters or information, or by asking a question of a large external group who may have useful information,or by scanning a bulletin board rich with related information. The power of that activity must be experienced to be appreciated. A review of several present users of these media may be helpful.

John Muffo of Virginia Polytechnic Institute and State University edits biweekly electronic mail newsletter for the Association for Institutional Research that reaches well over 600 respondents throughout the United States, Canada, Europe, and the Far East. I initiated a similar newsletter for the Society for College and University Planning, which is now edited by Joanne Cate at the University of California; it comes out every week or ten days and reaches about 500 subscribers. These newsletters include news of the association, conference announcements and calls for papers, queries to the readership on a wide variety of topics, the responses received to earlier queries, notes on useful publications or references, comments on questions of concern to the profession or to higher education in general, and other matters of interest. Other newsletters include CCNEWS, published by Wendy Rickard Bolletin of EDUCOM, which focuses on information about developments in information technology and newsletter editing, and NETMONTH, edited by Chris Condon through Yale University, which deals with news and issues affecting BITNET and related networks. A wide variety of other newsletters exist on topics ranging from offbeat humor to MacIntosh software and psychology.

The use of electronic mail discussion lists for higher education administration is growing rapidly. The Higher Education Data Sharing Consortium (HEDS) started one in February 1989. Six months later, about 50 of the 125 member institutions had connected, and the number continues to expand. Queries to date have ranged over topics as diverse as compensation for faculty department chairs; faculty teaching loads; the percentage of each class that has graduated with honors, by level and gender; the status of admissions applications; the manpower and space of registrars' offices; and the design of survey instruments for graduate students. In a similar fashion, members of the AAU Data Exchange make extensive use of CONFER, an electronic conferencing system offered by the University of Michigan. A discussion list for those interested in data administration (DASIG) has been started by Richard Sheeder at Penn State and Sue Borel at Syracuse University. The California regional AIR association has CAIRNet. Those interested in assessment issues can join AssessNet, produced by Mark Dubin at the University of Colorado–Boulder. Those interested in facilities and services have their own group, called FACSER, supported by Kate Bingham at West Virginia University. Other lists available through BITNET cover topics that range from atmospheric research to science fiction.

There are a number of formal data exchange consortia throughout the country, including AAUDE, HEDS, the Consortium on Financing Higher Education (COFHE), MINDS (for Methodist-related schools),

SUG for (Southern public universities), and SHEEO (for state higher education executive officers). While most of these consortia continue to collect their information in traditional paper and mail surveys, they are exploring ways of using electronic media to collect and disseminate results.

Disadvantages

Lest the reader conclude that I am a blind enthusiast for electronic communication, it should be noted that these media present their own problems. Electronic mail can be wonderful for time shifting, but it breaks down if your correspondent does not log in to his or her computer. Electronic mail is not yet sufficiently well established that everyone reads and answers mail quickly and routinely. The system works well only where it is used fairly heavily and regularly. To help accustom its members to the use of electronic mail, one consortium made a major point of requiring all participants to dial in to their electronic bulletin board at least once a week.

Data overload is another concern. Piles of data do not necessarily produce information. Junk mail on the networks is occasionally a problem, but it can usually be dealt with by a gentle remainder to the sender that the academic networks are intended for scholarly and administrative purposes. Legislation is in progress in several states and at the federal level to limit junk fax mail.

Another problem associated with the relative newness of electronic media is that it still requires altogether too much technical know-how to conduct routine business. Setting up mailing lists, getting people's electronic mail addresses, finding your way through the thicket of networks, even dealing with the complexities of your own institution's mail system can all be annoying and frustrating. The good news is that the networks are beginning to merge, better documentation is becoming available, and aids for the nontechnical newcomer are being developed.

It also needs to be understood that, while the individual message cost for electronic mail may be negligible, there is a time cost. Editing an electronic mail journal for a professional society took one editor at least an hour a day. A hazard of all new technologies is that they become intoxicating. One can spend disproportionate amounts of time playing on the machine and lose sight of the objective of providing data for decisions.

Finally, the multiplication of data access intensifies the problem of assuring the validity of the data. When everyone can and does contact his or her colleagues to find out what is going on elsewhere, it is not surprising that what emerges is not a single clear story but multiple, possibly confusing stories.

Some Guidelines for Effective Electronic Mail Survey Use

Mark Meredith (1989) suggests that the electronic mail user "may be rapidly overwhelmed by (1) requests from his/her own administration to do peer data gathering and/or (2) requests from other associations and colleagues. The user must strive for two kinds of balance: first, the total time/effort that goes into electronic exchange; second, a fair quid pro quo between give and take, so that the user is not mostly taking from others and not mostly giving data to others." He suggests six guidelines that can make e-mail surveys more effective.

First to get optimum data, the electronic mail user should draft all queries carefully; use clear definitions, terms, time periods, and so on; and simplify the request to the essential elements. It can be helpful to review your stated request in draft form with key people who want the data to give them a chance to clarify what they expect. Clear and simple requests get faster responses from more contacts.

Second, the person doing the electronic mail queries will almost always have to summarize the detailed, actual responses into concise, readable, understandable information that can be conveyed to executive officers and other users of institutional research. Be sure to keep this work load factor in mind. Note that the greater the detail and more complex the query, the greater will be the requirement to reduce the data for executive use.

Third, remember the collegial golden rule of data exchange: provide data to others as you would have them provide data to you.

Fourth, if possible, use a form of electronic mail that makes it easy to archive and retrieve queries and their responses. Some e-mail systems are available that build these features into the software.

Fifth, be selective about the electronic mail networks that you get into. Be cautious about multiple networks because of the possibility that you will receive too many requests for your data.

Last, be selective in the institutions and colleagues to whom you send your requests for data. Avoid the shotgun approach of asking everyone who is on the network. Direct your queries to a manageable number of institutions similar to yours. Better yet, consider establishing an electronic mail network for your designated or desired comparison group of institutions and get those involved to recognize the mutual benefit concept of participating.

Parting Advice

The institutional researcher should be alert to the ways in which information can be used so as to understand the situation in which he or she is asked for information and be able to provide what is appropriate.

Information can be used to provoke a decision or prepare the way for one by showing dissonance between prior concept or worldview and new information; to shape a decision by providing a context (for example, what the competition is doing), or by establishing the ranges within which decision can be made, or by quantifying alternatives, and so forth; to test a decision in cases where the decision maker pretty well knows what he or she wants to do and will go ahead with unless data show why, and where, and how that road presents difficulties; to rationalize and justify in cases where the decision maker seeks facts that bolster the case and help explain it to others; or to beat down opponents.

The data provider needs to recognize that data are never nonpolitical, never free from values. Data can be apposite, correct, and comprehensive, but judgments about the information to ask for, the interpretations that are made, and the ways in which they are presented are political as well as professional. Data will be used in different ways by different managers at different times. Data may be plentiful, but they are unlikely to be complete; for example, you may have data on eleven of the twenty institutions needed for a comparison. Data are always partial, only somewhat relevant, or both; for example, you may have data on family incomes for aid recipients but not for all families. Worst of all, the relevant data are in your files, not in the decision maker's head at the time when they are needed, because you did not know that she needed them then.

Having examined the pros and cons of electronic media, some characteristics of senior administrative decision making, and some challenges facing the data provider, what can we now say by way of advice to institutional researchers? What can the information provider do with electronic media to try to make information as useful as possible?

First, build an archive both of information and, perhaps more important, of rapidly available information sources. Those information sources can now include colleagues at other institutions, electronic bulletin boards, and discussion lists as well as tests and files kept in the office. A bit of information that can be provided while the caller is on the phone (or at least within the same day) is valuable and will be used, even if it is partial; it is better than systematic information provided a month after the decision.

Second, since many decisions are shaped by a variety of direct and indirect information inputs as they evolve, provide a context for information. As you build the archive, keep sending short interesting reports to key people. The reports can, of course, be electronic or paper. Some will not be timely, but you need to keep building their context. Then, when they make decisions, they will either have something in the back of their minds, or they may remember to call you.

Third, anticipate information needs wherever possible. For decisions that are cyclical, such as faculty salary setting, you can be prepared. You may be able to anticipate others if you know what is going on in the institution, among your peers, and in the outside world. (Are there likely to be legislative budget recisions? What is happening to the debt levels of medical students? Are applications for undergraduate admission up or down this year among your competitors?) Electronic mail newsletters, bulletin boards, and discussion lists are remarkably useful ways of keeping in touch with trends elsewhere and of accumulating useful information quickly.

Finally, explore the electronic media vigorously, and keep in touch with new developments. That world is changing very rapidly. It is now possible to access some remote data base systems and library catalogue via Internet and certain applications of LISTSERV and remote SPIRES via BITNET (St. George, 1989). By the time this chapter reaches print, it may also be possible to access remote data bases of useful institutional information, although where and how that will be done first is not clear as I write. While the technology is becoming more complex and sophisticated, it is also slowly becoming simpler for the nontechnical person to use. The costs of connection and use are significant, but so are the benefits.

References

Dunn, J. A., Jr. "Organizational Decision Making." In W. C. Swap and Associates (eds.), *Group Decision Making*. Newbury Park, Calif.: Sage, 1984.

Ewell, P. T., and Chaffee, E. E. "Promoting the Effective Use of Information in Decision Making." Paper research at the 24th annual forum of the Association for Institutional Research, Fort Worth, May 1984.

Meredith, M. Electronic mail correspondence, June 15, 1989 and July 3, 1989.

St. George, A. "Internet-Accessible Library Catalogs and Databases." Electronic mail transmission to Network Site Liaison list, May 19, 1989.

Simon, H. A. *Administrative Behavior*. New York: Macmillan, 1961.

Updegrove, D. A., "CCNews: A Wire Service for the Wired Campus." *EDUCOM Review*, Spring 1989a, pp. 55–57.

Updegrove, D. A. "What Is Electronic Mail and How Does It Work?" Working papers for "Electronic Mail as a Tool in Institutional Research and Planning." *AIR Professional File*, Tallahassee, Fla.: AIR, May 1989b.

John A. Dunn, Jr., is vice-president for planning at Tufts University and president of the Society for College and University Planning in 1989-90.

Lessons on information use can be summarized by a series of diagnostic questions, each of which should be answered before any information is communicated.

Putting It All Together: Four Questions for Practitioners

Peter T. Ewell

Practicing institutional researchers who have read thus far can perhaps be forgiven for being depressed. As every author has indicated, good analysis and good decisions are not necessarily related, and the seemingly straightforward process of providing sound information for decision makers is layered with complexity. At the same time, most readers will find much that is familiar in these discussions. Indeed, each reader will probably be able to supply multiple anecdotes that amply illustrate the many points made. What, then, do these discussions add up to?

First, they provide a systematic introduction to a diverse set of topics that affect information use but that are rarely presented together. Some chapters provide a point of entry into a rich and varied research literature, little of which may be familiar to practicing institutional researchers. Others provide detail on a particular problem area or informational application. Our intent in these chapters has been to provide a sourcebook. The references provided with the chapters are as important as the syntheses that they contain. At the same time, the volume considered as a whole suggests some broad lessons for practice. These lessons can, I think, be summarized by four diagnostic questions that institutional

P. T. Ewell (ed.). *Enhancing Information Use in Decision Making.*
New Directions for Institutional Research, no. 64. San Francisco: Jossey-Bass, Winter 1989.

researchers should apply in any attempt to generate and communicate action information.

Who's Asking?

All six chapters highlight the importance of knowing the decision maker. Every request for information (the same applies to unsolicited reports) should thus begin with a brief but rigorous analysis of the information client that addresses, at minimum, three issues: the perceptual style of the intended user, the user's sophistication with respect to information, and the user's place in the institution.

The User's Perceptual Style. As Hackman suggests, different individuals have different ways of looking at information. If the information is intended for a single decision maker or a small group of users, try to determine what is known about their preferences. What has been the fate of prior data-rich communications? Do they like numbers or pictures, or do they want the data to be described in words as well? How oriented are they likely to be to the bottom line or lower right-hand corner? Most important of all may be their disciplinary background. Most academic leaders will find information most appealing if it is consistent with their own past training and practice.

The User's Sophistication. Nothing is likely to be so futile as supplying administrators with arcane statistics that they are ill equipped and less inclined to deal with. At the same time, users who are highly sophisticated will fault analyses that appear to be overly simplistic or statistically inappropriate. As Jones and others suggest, a good first rule of presentation is Simple Is Best. However, this rule should not be taken as meaning that appropriate methods and analyses should be avoided. Powerful methods can be used to discover implications that can then be communicated in simple language. If sophisticated users require detail, it is available for further discussion.

The User's Place in the Institution. As the McLaughlins indicate, organizational position is critical in determining information requirements. What is the user's position in the decision-making structure, both informal and formal? Is he or she located in the same reporting line as the information supplier, and how far up or down? What lines of communication is he or she a part of, and what independent sources of information are available? Answers to each question may help to establish a context for communication and determine the likelihood that any information supplied will be taken seriously. At the same time, organizational position will partially dictate a set of preferences and interests regarding desired decisional outcomes. What are the user's preconceptions about the "answer" contained in the information supplied? Sorting through these issues may help the researcher to devise an information strategy that guards against premature dismissal or that makes deliberate misinterpretation more difficult.

Finally, as Borden and Delaney remind us, the *who* can be a group subject to each of the analyses just outlined, both as a group and independently as individual members. Furthermore, if the group is dispersed, new technologies such as e-mail or data sharing may be useful, as Jack Dunn suggests. And, Jones emphasizes, if the information supplier is part of the group, he or she may thus participate directly in making the decision. In each case, the strategies of communication and analysis will need to differ.

What For?

Cutting across the diagnosis of the user should be a parallel analysis of the intended use. As noted in Chapter One, the primary issue facing the user can be one of choosing among alternative actions, setting contexts, pointing out anomalies that might signal the presence of problems promoting closure on an issue, or selling a decision that has already been made to those who remain unconvinced. In each case, though the substantive topic addressed may be the same, the format and medium in which the information is supplied may decisively differ. This section addresses four other issues that may be important: the levels of decisions that are affected, the phase of decision, what is at stake, and whether the data are to be manipulated further.

The Levels of Decisions. The McLaughlins note three distinct kinds of decision processes—strategic, managerial, and operational—and document the manner in which information use differs among them. Differences are apparent here regarding appropriate source, timeliness, degree and level of analysis, and appropriate presentational format. Determining in advance the kinds of decision processes that supplied information will enter is therefore critical to effective communication.

The Phase of Decision. Regardless of the level of the decision process, potential decision situations can differ with respect to cycle or closure. Some situations may be close to resolution when the supplied information arrives; others may not have reached the point of determining the available alternatives. As both Jones and Dunn point out, the timing and phases of many such situations—for example, budget cycles and accreditation reviews—are known, and their information requirements may be anticipated. But, in many other situations, the analyst may need to assess carefully what phase the potential decision is in if the analyst is to supply the most useful information.

What Is at Stake. Information requirements can also vary as a result of the stakes associated with particular decisional outcomes. When much is at stake (or when much is perceived to be at stake), the information provided may need to serve the dual purpose of informing decision and of persuading all parties that the decision is well taken. As I noted in Chapter One, in such cases, methodological soundness and face validity become critical, because opposition is most likely to take shape as critiques of the information itself. Different decisional stakes may also dictate the levels of confidence with which information can be credibly advanced. Sensitivity analyses, in which the degree to which decisional outcomes remain unaffected over a determined range of probable informational variation, can be of particular value here.

Whether the Data Are to Be Manipulated Further. As both Jones and Borden and Delaney point out, institutional research is increasingly being called upon to supply "semifinished" data for others to manipulate with microcomputer data bases and spreadsheets. In such cases, ensuring common data definitions and data integrity is crucial. At the same time, it may be part of the information supplier's responsibility to provide technical support in the form of instruction about how to use the data properly and how to interpret the results obtained.

What's the Proper Medium?

The authors of all six chapters emphasize that the choice of a proper format and mode of communication is vital if the information supplied is to be used effectively. At minimum, institutional researchers should consider two distinct dimensions here. The first is how supplied data are to be presented visually—in graphic form, as words, or as numbers. Inside this issue, as Hackman emphasizes, are further choices about the proper chunking, the level of disaggregation or detail, and the types of data that are to be presented together. The second dimension is the medium used for communication—written, oral, or electronic. Here again, choices must be made about such further issues as relative ease of use, formality of the decision setting, or need for iterative discussion of results. In both cases, three issues deserve consideration: credibility and face validity, ease of use, and the degree of interpretation provided.

Credibility and Face Validity. In order to be used, the supplied information must not only be right but also look right. As a result, the levels of disaggregation used and the analytical detail provided should be tailored carefully to anticipate methodological objections. Results of sample-based studies or the use of complex statistical procedures may be particularly suspect in this regard, and precautions should be taken accordingly.

Ease of Use. As Dunn points out, the advantages of quick turnaround and dispersed communication that electronic media afford have corresponding disadvantages in requirements for high levels of technical facility and positive attitudes toward technology among potential users. In many cases, the use of such media is unwarranted because potential users will simply not take the trouble to learn the required procedures. These considerations are amplified when information is supplied to a group. In such cases, it is generally wise to tailor the medium to the level of technical proficiency of its least sophisticated member.

Degree of Interpretation Provided. The choice of medium can also be influenced by the amount of documentation or interpretation supplied. For interinstitutional data sharing, as Dunn notes, electronic communication media are ideal. The iterative capability of electronic media can also help a group to reach consensus on a conclusion. But, such media are less useful in presenting recommendations or the results of analyses. The most helpful alternative here may be an array of competing decision alternatives, each presented with its associated costs and benefits.

Finally, as Jones reminds us, it is important to separate the need for tailored communication from the requirements of sound research design and data analysis. Regardless of the style and content of the communication itself, the information that is supplied must always in principle be consistent with the formal canons of research reporting.

What Happens Next?

All six chapters emphasize that information use is not a series of independent incidents but an ongoing process. In many cases, the supplied information becomes the occasion for opening a dialogue rather than for reaching a decision. In other cases, varying interpretations can result from a series of analyses and counteranalyses drawn from the same data base and intended to support opposing points of view. Thus, in supplying information for decision, institutional researchers should always attempt to visualize the next steps. What will be the probable reactions of those to whom the information is supplied? Will greater detail be required in the form of further data disaggregation or further explanations of the methods used? Will opposing parties request analyses in response, and what is their character and content likely to be? Three issues need to be considered here: appropriate next moves, costs and technical requirements, and need for iteration.

Appropriate Next Moves. On each occasion that information is supplied, capacities for responding to anticipated further queries should be reviewed. What are the elements most likely to raise questions or objections? How well can these bet met, given the available data? In group settings, it may be appropriate to consider co-opting technically sophisticated group members to serve as data interpreters or advocates. In all situations, it may be appropriate to recognize that some battles are not worth fighting and consider walkaway points beyond which responses are unproductive, as the McLaughlins suggest.

Costs and Technical Requirements. Often, the appropriate next moves are strongly conditioned by the resources available. In anticipating further requests, information suppliers should also be prepared to cost them out roughly. It may be particularly appropriate for the needs of decision makers in this regard to consider the opportunity costs: what will not get done or be delayed as a consequence of further analysis?

Need for Iteration. Many decisions, especially group decisions, are not taken all at once. Rather, they are the product of several discussion iterations, each of which may require additional information. For relatively unformed decisions that are at an early stage of discussion, it may be inappropriate to supply all the information that is available and relevant. Rather, a small number of salient general indicators should be provided, each of which might provide a way into the issue under consideration. As Hackman notes, too much detail at this point may prove more confusing than helpful. And, as Borden and Delaney point out, as the size and diversity of the group increase, the number of iterations required to reach consensus will also increase.

Above all, in considering the next steps, institutional researchers should heed the advice of several authors in this sourcebook by considering their primary responsibility to be custodians of a data base. Increasingly, available information and technical sophistication are driving analysis to the local-user level. Here, information professionals are fulfilling a newer role of supplying raw or semifinished data to multiple users and actively coordinating a range of diverse institutional research functions across the campus. In such situations, such requirements as those suggested by Borden and Delaney for a chief information methodologist are critical.

Conclusion

Posing and answering each of these four questions can help institutional researchers in beginning to diagnose the informational consequences of different kinds of decision situations. Because institutional researchers will continue to be faced with an escalating variety of such situations, very different answers can be expected of this exercise each time it is applied; no one approach will work in all cases. Promoting the effective use of information in decision making remains an art, but it can surely be improved by renewed attention to some time-honored principles. We hope, in this regard, that this volume will be of service.

Peter T. Ewell is a senior associate at the National Center for Higher Education Management Systems (NCHEMS).

Index

A

AAU Data Exchange (AAUDE), 80
Academic decisions: and the anchoring and adjustment heuristic, 38-39; and the availability heuristic, 37; and the representativeness heuristic, 37-38
Adams, C. R., 3, 4, 9, 17
Adelman, L., 39, 48
Administrative cabinets, and research reports, 67
Administrative decision making, 76-78, 83-84
Administrative managers, and research reports, 66
Anderson, B. L., 43, 47
ANOVA, 66-67
Anthony, R. N., 21, 33
AssessNet, 80
Astin, A. W., 10, 18, 39, 47
Attitudes, shaping research reports, 65-66

B

Baldridge, J. V., 1, 4, 10, 18
Bargaining activities, and information barriers, 31-32
Barriers to information use, a framework of, 23
Beskamp, L. A., 15
BITNET, 58, 76, 79-80
Boruch, R. F., 10-11, 18
Boucher, W. I., 26, 33
Braskamp, L. A., 1, 2, 4, 17, 18-19
Brown, R. D., 2, 4, 17, 18-19
Brown, R. E., 1, 4, 15, 18
Brunsson, N., 1, 4, 13, 18
Buhl, L. C., 9, 18
Bullen, C. V., 32, 33

C

CAIRnet, 80
California regional AIR association, 80

Campbell, D. T., 8, 18
CCNEWS, 80
Chaffee, E. E., 1, 4, 10, 12, 18, 52-53, 58, 77, 84
Chief information officer (CIO), and institutional researchers, 56-57
Chircop, S., 11, 19
Churchman, C. W., 11, 18
COBOL, 69
Coleman, J. S., 1, 2, 4
Computer models, 57; and academic decision making, 39-40
Computerized information, capturing, 24
Computerized research reports, 63-64
CONFER, 75-76, 80
Corrigan, B., 39, 47

D

DASIG, 80
Data administration (DA), 24
Data base administration (DBA), 24
Data chunking, 40-41
Data users, and research reports, 66-67
Dawes, R. M., 39, 47
Decision maker characteristics, in information use, 16-17
Decision makers: understanding, 41-42. See also Information users
Decision making, 11-12; administrative, 83-84; and electronic media, 76-78; and information use, 11-12; and negative evidence, 45-47; and new hypotheses, 45-47. See also Group decision making
Decision-making models, of organizational process, 10
Decisions: data and, 88; levels of, 87; phase of, 87; stakes associated with, 87-88
DeLong, D. W., 32, 33
Deming, W. E., 55, 56, 58
DeSanctis, G., 49, 54, 58
Desktop publishing, 69

U.S. Postal Service

STATEMENT OF OWNERSHIP, MANAGEMENT AND CIRCULATION
Required by 39 U.S.C. 3685

1A. Title of Publication	1B. PUBLICATION NO.	2. Date of Filing
New Directions for Institutional Re-search	0 9 8 - 8 3 0	10/27/89

3. Frequency of Issue	3A. No. of Issues Published Annually	3B. Annual Subscription Price
quarterly	4	$42 individual $56 institutional

4. Complete Mailing Address of Known Office of Publication (Street, City, County, State and ZIP+4 Code) (Not printers)

350 Sansome Street, San Francisco, CA 94104-1310

5. Complete Mailing Address of the Headquarters of General Business Offices of the Publisher (Not printer)

(above address)

6. Full Names and Complete Mailing Address of Publisher, Editor, and Managing Editor (This item MUST NOT be blank)

Publisher (Name and Complete Mailing Address)

Jossey-Bass Inc., Publishers (above address)

Editor (Name and Complete Mailing Address)

Patrick T. Terenzini, Institute of Higher Education, Candler Hall, University of Georgia, Athens, GA 30602

Managing Editor (Name and Complete Mailing Address)

Steven Piersanti, President, Jossey-Bass Inc., Publishers (above address)

7. Owner (If owned by a corporation, its name and address must be stated and also immediately thereunder the names and addresses of stockholders owning or holding 1 percent or more of total amount of stock. If not owned by a corporation, the names and addresses of the individual owners must be given. If owned by a partnership or other unincorporated firm, its name and address, as well as that of each individual must be given. If the publication is published by a nonprofit organization, its name and address must be stated.) (Item must be completed.)

Full Name	Complete Mailing Address
Maxwell Communications Corp., plc	Headington Hill Hall
	Oxford OX30BW
	U.K.

8. Known Bondholders, Mortgagees, and Other Security Holders Owning or Holding 1 Percent or More of Total Amount of Bonds, Mortgages or Other Securities (If there are none, so state)

Full Name	Complete Mailing Address
none	

9. For Completion by Nonprofit Organizations Authorized To Mail at Special Rates (DMM Section 423.12 only)
The purpose, function, and nonprofit status of this organization and the exempt status for Federal income tax purposes (Check one)

(1) Has Not Changed During Preceding 12 Months	(2) Has Changed During Preceding 12 Months	(If changed, publisher must submit explanation of change with this statement.)

10. Extent and Nature of Circulation	Average No. Copies Each Issue During Preceding 12 Months	Actual No. Copies of Single Issue Published Nearest to Filing Date
A. Total No. Copies (Net Press Run)	1600	1674
B. Paid and/or Requested Circulation 1. Sales through dealers and carriers, street vendors and counter sales	162	25
2. Mail Subscription (Paid and/or requested)	905	1004
C. Total Paid and/or Requested Circulation (Sum of 10B1 and 10B2)	1067	1029
D. Free Distribution by Mail, Carrier or Other Means Samples, Complimentary, and Other Free Copies	205	185
E. Total Distribution (Sum of C and D)	1272	1214
F. Copies Not Distributed 1. Office use, left over, unaccounted, spoiled after printing	328	460
2. Return from News Agents		
G. TOTAL (Sum of E, F1 and 2—should equal net press run shown in A)	1600	1674

11. I certify that the statements made by me above are correct and complete

Signature and Title of Editor, Publisher, Business Manager, or Owner

Vice-President

PS Form 3526, Feb. 1989 (See instructions on reverse)